Days of Hope Confidently & Joyfully

A Healing Journey through Depression

D1115673

Chaundra A. Rush

All Bible references are taken from the New Living Translation unless otherwise noted.
New Living Translation, Bible Gateway. Web. (Oct 2012)
Peterson, Eugen H. The Message. Bible Gateway. Web. (25 Oct 2012)
Editor: Penelope Hughes

ISBN: 1499132360
ISBN-13: 9781499132366

Acknowledgements

To MY HUSBAND who has always stood by me and saw my potential, despite my illness.

To my daughters (Charaia, Shaina and Anisha) who always made good choices and have incredible young women of God who never became bitter even though life with "Bipolar Mom" can get pretty confusing at times. My sons are just as gentle and kind as their Dad.

To my parents whose prayers continue to sustain me along with their highest hopes and dreams for me.

To Janet who has always stood beside me as a great friend, confident, accountability and prayer partner throughout all the years of weekly Sunday conversations.

To Bobbie who was willing to walk a desperate woman through the darkest days of her life and who has been such a mentor and example of a godly wife and mother.

To Jesus Christ who is the Author and Finisher of my faith, my God, my Healer and my Friend. All the glory belongs to You.

Introduction

FIRST OFF, I would like to apologize.

This book is full of mistakes. You may find typos, formatting issues, margin errors, etc. But I submitted this manuscript anyway as a demonstration of how we can get so hung up on the details and perfection that we are paralyzed and the truth we have to offer might die with us and never be shared. So as you read, I pray you see truth and not perfection and the message that there is not such thing as perfect people. We are all on the same path of just being ourselves by the grace of God.

What does it mean to be a Believer who struggles with depression or mental illness? What happens when a person who believes in God, has faith in Jesus Christ as Lord literally loses their mind? What does God say about clinical depression? Does He consider us weak-minded or lazy? I don't believe He condemns us, even if, for some reason, we caused it ourselves through neglect of our bodies. As our Creator He knows our bodies and how our brain functions, as well as, what the root cause of our depression. He can heal us and bring wholeness to our body, mind and spirit. We are three-part beings – spirit, soul and body. Although we have to attend to our spiritual well-being, we are not just spiritual beings who float around communing with God without taking care of our physical and emotional well-being which ultimately effects our health and wellness.

I was 21 when I had my first psychotic episode. I had been wandering around our apartment complex in my father's shirt, my coat and no shoes. I was knocking on doors to witness to residents about Jesus Christ and someone called the police. It was 2 a.m. in the morning and I had no concept of where I was or what was happening to me. Someone called the police and I was handcuffed and taken to my parents' house by the Palmdale/Lancaster Sheriff. I was then involuntarily admitted into a mental health hospital. This is where my treatment of depression and Schizoaffective Bipolar I Disorder began.

Schizoaffective disorder is a condition in which a person experiences a combination of schizophrenia symptoms - such as hallucinations or delusions — and mood disorder symptoms, such as mania or depression.[1]

I was in the hospital for three weeks. Because of my shame (and spiritual pride), I refused to take the medication they wanted to give me. I distinctly remember some very bitter cranberry juice as I slowly came back to reality. I was in psychosis for almost two weeks.

As a born-again Christian, it was difficult for me to resolve what was happening to me because of all I had been taught about sickness, healing and, most of all, the stigma surrounding depression and mental illness. I have finally come to the point where I think of this illness and others like it, such as, Post Traumatic Stress Disorder (PTSD), Attention Deficit Hyperactivity Disorder (ADHD), Major Depression, Clinical Depression, Bipolar I and II the same as any other ailment such as Diabetes, Multirole Sclerosis (MS) or even cancer. It's a condition that causes many levels of mental, emotional and physical suffering and is very debilitating. The good news is that God can heal us at the very core of our beliefs in His own time and in His own way, not ours.

The most painful moment of my recovery was admitting I had a diagnosis. In effect, it was the same as admitting that something was wrong with my pancreas and needed to be treated for it. I also had to realize that my recovery was a process as well as an event The event was when I gave my life to Christ. The process is unlearning false beliefs and learning the knowledge of the Truth. We would like it to be an event that ended all. And, it is through the cross of Jesus Christ who promised that we would laid hands on the sick and they would recover. The key word here is recover which means to regain health after sickness; to change; to mend;to grow well. It is a process.

Society, and sometimes the Church, often sees depression as a weakness, a character flaw or a lack of faith. The media portrays those with any kind of mental disorder as criminals or homeless, which continues to feed the stigma attached to the disease or condition.

When it comes to our faith in Jesus Christ, we are so much more than our symptoms.

"Can anything ever separate us from Christ's love? Does it mean he no longer loves us if we have trouble or calamity...No, despite all these things, overwhelming victory is ours through Christ, who loved us. And I am convinced that nothing can ever separate us from God's love. Neither death nor life, neither angels nor demons, neither our fears for today nor our worries about tomorrow—not even the powers of hell can separate us from God's love. No power in the sky above or in the earth below—indeed, nothing in all creation will ever be able to separate us from the love of God that is revealed in Christ Jesus our Lord" (Rom. 8.35, 37-39).

We are worth so much more to God than death or life or things in the earth or in Heaven or angels or demons. Nothing can separate us from His love. Our value to Him is our lives and only our lives. We overcome only through His love for us and not through anything we have done. We have to believe in Him and not in what He can do for us. Our faith lies in His sacrifice alone, not in our faith in Him. We shouldn't have faith in our faith, then we would think everything happened because of our effort or our prayers. When Jesus is Lord of our lives, we give Him sovereignty in all the affairs of our life. We surrender our lives to Him, even through unanswered prayer. We trust in His word and His sovereignty. We have to trust His character, who He really is, as well as, His power.

So many of us who struggle with mental illness or depression often struggle in our faith during those times, as would anyone who was experiencing any level of suffering. But I have learned that through the struggles and my times of weakness my faith has been made stronger. We can endure through each trial because, contrary to popular belief, trials develop character. One of my favorite scriptures reminds me of one of the purposes for trials in our life.

"We can rejoice, too, when we run into problems and trials, for we know that they help us develop endurance. And endurance develops strength of character, and character strengthens our confident hope of salvation. And this hope will not lead

to disappointment. For we know how dearly God loves us, because he has given us the Holy Spirit to fill our hearts with his love" (Rom. 5.3-5).

We have heard it said in Christian circles that we don't want to go around the same mountain or through the same test again and again. Thankfully, Jesus is a teacher and teaches us as many times as it takes for us to get what He wants to teach us into our hearts eternally. Each time around the mountain of depression I got stronger. The landscape looked the same, but each time the Lord taught me something about me and about Him that I didn't know before the trial. His patience is unending, so Satan's goal is to get us to give up on ourselves.

I experienced years of cycles of depression and there's one thing I learned: It is not the number of cycles I go through that matters as much getting up after each one. And I intend to keep getting up should I find myself there again.

Satan is the enemy of our faith in God and our flesh and our will constantly fights against the Spirit of God who lives in us.

"For the sinful nature is always hostile to God. It never did obey God's laws, and it never will" (Rom. 8.7).

In the natural, we still have a physical body that houses our spirit and soul. Our brain houses our mind will and emotions. Researching my illness gave me wisdom, knowledge and understanding. It helped me to become a part of the treatment process. If we had cancer, we would look at different forms of treatment and all of our options. Yet, when it comes to this illness or symptoms of depression, we sometimes stay in denial about it, hoping it will just go away.

Some symptoms of depression include:

- Difficulty concentrating, remembering details, and making decisions
- Fatigue and decreased energy
- Feelings of guilt worthlessness, and/or helplessness
- Feelings of hopelessness and/or pessimism

℘ Insomnia, early-morning wakefulness, or excessive sleeping

℘ Irritability, restlessness

℘ Loss of interest in activities or hobbies once pleasurable, including sex (for all you married folks)

℘ Overeating or appetite loss

℘ Persistent aches or pains, headaches, cramps, or digestive problems that do not ease even with treatment

℘ Persistent sad, anxious, or "empty" feelings

℘ Thoughts of suicide, suicide attempts

It is because of all these symptoms that I have written this book. I know what it's like to feel helpless, hopeless, empty and lonely. I try to address some of these symptoms and encourage you through and some of the lies that go through your mind. I would like to help you focus on the truth of what God says about us without any judgment or condemnation. And, I would count it an absolute honor and privilege for the opportunity to walk through this with you in some way.

Spiritually, we know the power of God lives in us and is greater than our sin. The Holy Spirit is able to keep us. But, we work together with Him. We have to do our part and He will supernaturally do His. We submit our will to Him and that's not easy when you are struggling in your thinking. When no matter how you try you are unable to focus on the Word of God, what He is saying or what anyone is saying to you. We can't just will ourselves better. We need to do what we have to do physically to keep ourselves healthy for God.

When we are suffering from depression, it is difficult to stay focused on one thing, especially any kind of scripture. Many well-meaning Christians will tell us to just read our Bible and pray not realizing how difficult, if not impossible, it is to do. What I would like to do in this book is to try to encourage you to keep your eyes on Jesus and help you to remember. So many times we forget and just need a gentle reminder of God's love and care for us. I also learned how to silently read my prayers. Yet, there were also times when I needed to hear myself read small passages of scripture, so I included short prayers and scripture at the end of each day.

There can be so many factors contributing to depression, which is why if we are suffering for more than two weeks, we should see a doctor. It could be caused by so many things: thyroid imbalances, hormones, blood sugar levels, lack of sleep, or any number of physical problems, including a malfunction in the brain that needs to be addressed.

For years I would not trust a doctor, especially when he recommended medication. Again, for me, it was spiritual pride because of the mindset I had about medication for depression. (Some think a person could become addicted to them.) This kept me from getting the help I needed to function better as a wife and mother of three (now five).

There are some things we can do naturally, and those treatments should be discussed with your doctor. Don't be afraid to work with him and your family about medications. I do suggest some exercises that may help with anxiety, stress or depression, but I am not a doctor and do not recommend you perform these without consulting your doctor. We need to use wisdom when it comes to our physical bodies, which affect our emotional and spiritual well-being.

Everyone's journey looks different. God works with each of us individually as we walk through our recovery process. I thought I would share mine in hopes that it will provide some relief from the hopelessness and despair you may be feeling right now. My prayer is that each day will be a gentle word of encouragement or reminder of God's goodness, grace and love for you.

You are not alone and God will never abandon you. The Holy Spirit knows how to pray for you and knows what you need to hear. I am trusting that you will hear Him praying for you through this book as I share my journey with you.

http://www.mayoclinic.org/diseases-conditions/schizoaffective-disorder/basics/definition/con-20029221

The Cast Down Sheep

"Why so cast down, O my soul? Why so disquieted within me?
Hope in God".

~P<small>SALMS</small> 42.5

P<small>SALM</small> 42 IS a Psalm of contemplation. It was written by a musician who ministered in the temple, a son of Korah. The questions he contemplates are, "How did I get here?" and "Why am I in this situation?"

It's interesting the author used "cast down" to describe his depression. When a sheep is carrying an unborn lamb, is too fat or its wool has become too heavy, it will seek a hollow or depression to rest. In the process they become "cast" which is when, somehow, their feet come off the ground, they roll over and their feet end up straight up in the air. What a helpless, hopeless place to be.

When we experience depression or a psychotic episode, our symptoms seem to have come out of nowhere. We find ourselves feeling helpless and hopeless, completely defenseless and at the mercy of our enemies. We ask ourselves, "Why?" "How did I get here?" "Why can't I get out, no matter how hard I try?" When we are "cast", we can't "will" ourselves better. Our feet are stuck straight up in the air and the only way out of our suffering is through Jesus our Shepherd. We can't "will" our way out of clinical depression and it's not our fault.

In Psalms 23, we see the rod and the staff. A shepherd's rod is used to count the sheep every night as they come in from pasture. The shepherd literally knows every sheep by name and if one is missing he will leave the ninety-nine to search for the lost one. He knows every second counts. That lost or cast sheep is open to predators and the elements.

When the shepherd gets to the sheep, he nurses it back to health. He takes care of ailments and then gently massages the legs so it can stand on its own and join the flock.

When we are suffering through depression we don't realize that Jesus comes immediately to our rescue. In most cases we just want out, right away. Jesus wants to minister to us and address the real causes behind us getting there. We feel like it is our fault when, actually, it is just the result of the natural process of being sheep. Jesus, our shepherd, never judges us, but lovingly and gently tends to us, right in the midst of our pain.

"Why am I so discouraged? Why is my heart so sad? I will put my hope in God! I will praise Him again — my Savior and my God? Now I am deeply discouraged, but I will remember you" (Ps. 42.5, 6).

Maybe the psalmist is familiar with shepherding and uses this picture of a sheep that is cast down to describe his feelings of helplessness and hopelessness. How he longs to see the face of his shepherd. How he longs to feel his nearness and comfort again. He puts his hope in God as he expectantly waits, knowing He will come to deliver him.

After the shepherd has mended his little sheep, he picks it up and carries it on his shoulder, taking him wherever he goes until his legs are strong enough. As he carries it, a bond is created and the sheep wants to go wherever the shepherd goes. He is seldom out of his sight. God's grace carries us during this time. It helps us get through each day and to keep waking up each morning. His Spirit comforts us and encourages us to continue to wait on God, through His word and through others. This creates a special intimacy with God where we know him and are used to being in his presence. A special bond is created through this time of suffering that you never want to be without again.

Psalms 23 shows how our shepherd tends to his sheep, one by one. It is one passage we can contemplate when we suffer through depression. Our goal is not to get ourselves out, but to wait on the one who will rescue us in his time and, when he does we will be stronger and closer to him than before. Our whole purpose in life should be to know Him in the power of His resurrection and the fellowship of His sufferings (Phil. 3.10).

Put your hope in God. Trust in Him. Allow Him to tend to you the way He chooses to during this dark season. It may mean medicine for a season. It may mean a sabbatical of some sort. However he wants to nurture you, allow him. Don't focus on how long, just know your change is going to come.

It is not through any fault of your own that you are in this place. God is with you and will reveal Himself to you through *everything*.

Prayer: Father, I will remember You and will wait expectantly for Your rescue. I will trust in what You have spoken and in what You say about me. I will worship You and recognize and thank You for being here with me always.

———

Affirmation
I will wait on You, O God. You are my strength, high tower and refuge. I hide myself in you throughout this storm.

———

Scriptures to meditate on:

"Do not turn your back on me. D o not reject your servant in anger. You have always been my helper. Don't leave me now; don't abandon me. O God of my salvation" (Ps. 27.9).

"Wait patiently for the LORD. Be brave and courageous. Yes, wait patiently for the LORD" (Ps. 27.14).

Get off the Treadmill

"Be still and know that I am God"

~Psalms 46.10

INTIMACY WITH GOD is four letters – S-T-O-P.

One of the hardest things to do these days is to be still. It is a lost art. We actually need to practice being still. I sometimes see myself as that guinea pig running on the treadmill, never stopping until I just topple over exhausted. I find myself on the treadmill of life wanting to jump off but too afraid and, yet knowing that if I don't, I will soon crash anyway. During those times, I go from home to daycare, to school to saxophone lessons, to church, then back home, cook dinner and on and on and on until I fall into bed exhausted only to start again the next morning.

Stress is a huge contributor to depression. In fact some researchers have found that lack of brain chemical Serotonin is not the only cause of depression, but also the increase of the stress hormone Cortisone. Stress is a huge trigger for me and being too busy is one of the main causes.

God gave us a Sabbath. He told us to work six days and on the seventh we should rest.

"You must keep the Sabbath day, for it is a holy day for you...You have six days each week for you ordinary work, but the seventh day must be a Sabbath day of complete rest, a holy day dedicated to the Lord..." (Exod. 31.14a, 15).

Jesus said that the Sabbath was made for us (Mark 2.27), yet we often squander it and don't recognize God made it for us. He even rested as an example for us on the seventh day.

"And on the seventh day God ended His work which He had done, and He rested on the seventh day from all His work which He had done" (Gen. 2.2)

We need a Sabbath - a day of rest. In today's society, though, it seems difficult to even take 15 minutes to rest, let alone a whole day. He is our example. If He took it, we should take it.

When we don't get enough sleep it can lead to chemical imbalances in our brain that can lead to depression. One way the body restores Serotonin in our brain is through sleep. Not just any sleep but a deep Rapid Eye Movement (REM) sleep. So one of the best ways to ward off depression is by getting enough sleep. Eight to nine hours is recommended.

In today's fast paced world it is difficult to learn how to be still and turn off your brain so you can sleep. In fact, when you are finally still and the house or car is quiet, you may find yourself getting a little nervous. Your thoughts wander and you find that it takes a while for your mind to be still even though your body is. For me, hectic days bring stress and can be disastrous.

When I am in a manic mood (a state of euphoria associated with Bipolar disorder) it is hard for me to concentrate and focus my thoughts. It is also easy to get so busy and do as many things as I can, thinking that I am invincible. I have to force myself to stop and be still when I am aware that I am manic. During those times when I am in my bed, late at night, "I commune with my own heart upon my own bed." (Ps. 4.4). I upload all of the information in my head up to the Lord as I wait on Him in silence. I focus specifically on the goodness of God and the attributes of God (i.e. You are so Mighty, Awesome, Powerful, Faithful, Loving and Kind, etc.) or I keep my mind from wandering by focusing on one single verse of scripture and think of different ways to say it.

Racing thoughts are a symptom of mania so this is especially difficult for me to do, but with practice I learned how to quiet my thoughts. To share what's on my heart and then take time to listen to what is on God's. By doing this, I enter into the true rest of the Lord and that secret place – His Sabbath.

The best way to practice this skill is to have quiet time in the morning before the day begins, or at the end of the day. Find a quiet place to do this. For me, it is a chair next to my bed with a lamp and table. I have my Bible, a notebook and pen. Sometimes I just sit and wait. Sometimes, my heart is so full that I have to write my prayers and thoughts. You will soon find it difficult to go a day without it.

When we were first placed with our two newly adopted sons, quiet time was a luxury that was few and far between. It still is at times. So I learned how to journal my prayers while I was sitting and watching them play. I would turn the radio off in the car when I ran errands (alone). I had to steal quick moments when the house was quiet. Don't get caught up in religious, rigid times. Snatch those moments and cherish them. Protect them. Recognize them. Enjoy them.

There are times when physiological changes have kicked in and my mind will not turn off because no matter how hard I try, even when my body is still, my brain is still processing. Some days I journal, others I listen to calm music and begin breathing slowly to bring my heart rate down and relieve some of the anxiety and stress. Breathing and focusing on the attributes of God and becoming aware of His nearness really helps me to get to a place where I can rest, even if I don't actually get to sleep for a while.

Practice being still. Simplify your life. Get off that treadmill and learn to enjoy some quiet time with the Lord. It is during those times that you will find His strength, peace and refreshment.

Prayer: Lord, help me to slow down enough to be still before You. Show me what is mine to do. Help me to prioritize my day so that You are first and that everything else is done through Your direction and guidance. In Jesus' name, Amen

———◆———

Affirmation
My soul thirsts after You like a deer pants for the water. You lead me beside still waters.

———◆———

Scriptures to meditate on:

"Then Jesus said, 'Come to me all of you who are weary and carry heavy burdens, and I will give you rest. Take my yoke upon you. Let me teach you, because I am humble and gentle at heart, and you will find rest for your souls. For my yoke is easy to bear, and the burden I give you is light'" (Matt. 11.28-30).

"He lets me rest in green meadows, he leads me beside peaceful streams" (Ps.23.2).

"The LORD replied, 'I will personally go with you, Moses, and I will give you rest — everything will be fine for you'" (Exod. 33.14).

Maintaining Ground

"The Lord your God will drive those nations out ahead of you little
by little. You will not clear them all away at once, otherwise the wild
animals will multiply too quickly for you".

~DEUTERONOMY. 7.22

FOR YEARS I wondered why I just couldn't wake up one morning and be healed. Why I couldn't just have an instantaneous miracle. All of us would choose to be healed that way but God's ways are higher than ours and He is infinite in wisdom. His ultimate goal is for us to be conformed into the image of His Son, Jesus Christ. (Rom. 8.29). Although there are times when healing is instantaneous, my healing is a process over time bringing physical, spiritual and emotional wholeness.

God told the Israelites that He would drive out all of their enemies little by little. He said that if He did it all at once, then the wild beasts would multiply too quickly.

"Little by little I will drive them out from before you, until you have increased,
and you inherit the land" (Exod. 23.30).

"And the LORD your God will drive out those nations before you little by little;
you will be unable to destroy them at once, lest the beasts of the field become too
numerous for you" (Deut. 7.22)

When I found this scripture, I realized that God was healing me little by little. He was strategically and deliberately giving me victory over all my enemies, which were thoughts that were contrary to what God said in His Word about me (and about Him). I trust God's wisdom in this. He said that if He delivered us all at once that it would be too difficult for us to maintain. I believe the process is deliverance, then maintenance, then go after more ground and maintain it, then go after more ground, and so on. We should maintain the healing we have already received in one area before He moves us on to another area of healing. In other words, be patient and give yourself some time.

I had an overwhelming fear of abandonment. I was constantly worried that I would be left behind when the Rapture took place. It constantly filled my thoughts. This was the source of many years of depression. Whenever I had a psychotic break, it became my reality. I was left behind and there was no hope for me. I was afraid that I was rejected by God and abandoned to fend for myself. When the Lord delivered me from the fear of abandonment and rejection through prayer with a counselor, I had to fill my heart with the Word of God and fortify that area which used to be a stronghold of the enemy. For weeks I studied about everything that came with my salvation. I had to remember and be mindful of much I was loved and accepted by God. Eventually, I was able to resist those thoughts that challenged me in the same area I had been freed of with the Word of God. It took a process of weeks of prayer for every area to be dealt with and with every piece of ground I gained I had to strengthen my heart with the Word of God so that I would not return to my old ways of thinking.

Maintaining our ground means walking out the Word of God daily and doing our best not to act on our fears. It means we begin to become who we believe we are in Christ as we change our way of thinking and begin to develop habits reflecting that change. It means we don't back down from God's promises. We should not back off of our confession of faith and we should fortify and strengthen what remains. We should remember all we have learned and continue to put it into practice or we will let them slip.

"So we must listen very carefully to the truth we have heard, or we may drift away from it" (Heb. 2.1).

Another example of this process is how a carpenter finishes furniture. First he strips it, sands it, coats it with varnish and lets it dry. Then he puts on another coat of varnish, but not until the previous coat has completely dried. Every process is done patiently. So it is with the Jesus, our Master Carpenter. He patiently goes through the finishing process until it is complete.

"And I am certain that God, who began the good work within you, will continue his work until it is finally finished on the day when Christ Jesus returns" (Phil. 1.6).

Day by day, little by little, the Lord is freeing us to serve Him better. He will complete the work He started in us. Our job is to remain expectant of God's complete deliverance. God will strengthen us and destroy all of our enemies of fear, guilt and shame. He's already destroyed them and done the work, we just want to see it demonstrated in our lives.

Prayer: Lord, prefect that which concerns me: Your mercy, O Lord endures forever. Forsake not the works of Your own hands (Ps. 138.8).

———◆———

Affirmation
The Lord will complete the work in me until the day of Jesus Christ. I am healed and delivered and renewed day by day (2 Cor. 4.16).

———◆———

Scriptures to meditate on:

"But I will not drive them out in a single year, because the land would become desolate and the wild animals would multiply and threaten you. I will drive them out a little at a time..." (Exod. 23.29, 30)

"But we all, with open face beholding as in a glass the glory of the Lord, are changed into the same image from glory to glory even as by the Spirit of the Lord" (2 Cor. 3.18)

Never Alone

"...for He [God] Himself has said, I will not in any way fail you nor give you up nor leave you without support. [I will] not, [I will] not, [I will] not in any degree leave you helpless nor forsake nor let [you] down (relax My hold on you)! [Assuredly not!]"

~HEBREWS. 13. 5, (AMP)

WHEN DEALING WITH depression it is easy to isolate yourself, because you feel utterly alone. You feel helpless and abandoned. You wonder, "Where is God? I don't feel Him close to me." Your inclination is to begin to think and act as though God has left you completely alone. You feel as empty as a drum, but nothing could be further from the truth. God is as close as your breath. He is just a prayer away. He will not leave you nor forsake you. His promises are true and He is faithful to them.

There were days when I felt as though I had fallen out of grace. As if I didn't have the strength to even believe any more. This is when God tightens His hold on you. That is when you have to know that though everyone else may leave, God has not left you. Even though you may not feel God's presence you need to know He is near. Begin speaking to Him and sharing your worries, your fears, your doubts and your hopes. Even the shortest prayer can be powerful because praying demonstrates your faith in knowing He hears you.

"And we are confident that he hears us whenever we ask for anything that pleases him. And since we know he hears us when we make our requests, we also know that he will give us what we ask for." (1 John 4.14, 15)

There was a season when I prayed short, desperate prayers all day long. It was the only way I could function. They were short one-sentence prayers, like, "Lord, please help me get through this traffic. Lord, please help me go shopping. Help me get out of this bed and get the kids to school." The more I prayed, the more aware I was of God's nearness to me and of His ability to help and support me. I was alone, but not alone. I didn't realize at the time that every time I turned and drew near to Him, he turned and drew near to me just as He promised (Jam. 4.8). I would sometimes pray short scriptures throughout the day. On days when I was particularly tormented with fear my scripture would be, "There is no fear in love. But perfect love casts out fear" (I John 4.18).

It wasn't enough to just quote scripture all day, I had to actually focus on what I was saying. I had to meditate on what that scripture meant. I had to know how much God loved me and then act on that love by believing He has everything in control and He cares for me. The more I prayed to Him, the closer He became, until I knew He truly was with me everywhere I went experientially, not just intellectually.

One definition of meditate is "to mutter, or ponder by talking to oneself". We are to meditate on God's word day and night.

"But they delight in the law of the Lord, meditating on it day and night" (Ps. 1.2)

Talking to yourself helps you get the Word of God deep down into your heart. It's why we need to be careful what we do say to ourselves. We need to make sure we are telling ourselves what God's word says about us instead of the lies of the enemy.

Another way God lets us know that He is near is through godly friendships. I have been blessed with godly friends who can even hear in my voice when I am struggling.

"Confess your faults one to another, and pray one for another, that you may be healed…"

(Jas. 5.14, KJV).

God always provides a safe place for us to confess our fears and doubts and receive prayer. It is part of the healing process. It is important to find a safe place through godly friendships. This doesn't mean you necessarily tell just anyone your business. It does mean to prayerfully consider pursuing a relationship with people you trust, gradually over time.

There is one friendship where I just asked her if I could meet her for lunch. I was going through a long period of depression. Nothing helped and in desperation, I looked through my address book and found Bobbie's name. I had only known Bobbie for two weeks. I met her when I trained her for a position I left. I called her for lunch and went to meet her at her job. To my embarrassment, I met her from time to time at church on Sundays, but besides that, I didn't interact with her much at all. When we met, I cried through the whole hour. Amazingly, she offered to have lunch with me once a week and we have been close friends ever since.

She helped me get through a difficult time in my life, but if I hadn't taken a chance I would have missed out on a truly God-sent friendship. I am thankful for God's faithfulness to provide godly friendships. If you don't have godly friends then find a Christian counselor who will pray with you.

I bring this friendship up because, before I made that phone call, I thought I could make it on my own by just spending extra time in prayer and reading my Bible. I was taught that if you reached out for a friend, that person would become a crutch instead of being completely dependent on God. This is so erroneous and I would not have made it had I stayed isolated in my house. Jesus never intended for us to walk this earth alone. If you will notice, He didn't do it when He was here. He took His time alone, but even when He was in the Garden of Gethsemane, He took Peter, James and John. On His way to Calvary, our loving Heavenly Father sent Simon to help Him bear the cross. What makes us think we can spend our time here on this earth void of relationships that will help us in times of difficulty? Jesus continually said He was dependent on the Father, yet His desire is for us to be one as He and the Father are one and to love one another. Don't be afraid to reach out. Don't believe the lie that you have less faith if you do. It simply isn't true.

So practice recognizing God's presence by speaking to Him throughout the day. Don't stop praying (I Thessalonians 5.17). Draw near to God and He will draw near to you. Know that He is near to you today and always through His Word and godly friendships. He will never leave you nor give up on you.

Prayer: Lord, I know that I am in the palm of your hand and that no one can pluck me out. Thank you for walking with me today. Let me feel Your presence day by day. Thank You for drawing close to me as I draw close to You. Show me godly people who will pray with me and stand with me. Thank you for godly friendships.

———————

Affirmation
I am not forsaken or forgotten!!

———————

Scriptures to meditate on:

"Once I was young, and now I am old. Yet I have never seen the godly abandoned or their children begging bread" (Ps. 37.25)

"I give them eternal life and they will never perish. No one can snatch them away from me, for my Father has given them to me, and he is more powerful than anyone else" (John 10.28, 29)

"After David had finished talking with Saul, he met Jonathan, the king's son. There was an immediate bond between them, for Jonathan loved David... And Jonathan made a solemn pact with David, because he loved him as he loved himself" (1 Sam. 18.1, 3)

"...And be sure of this, I am with you always, even to the end of the age" (Matt. 28.20b).

Godly Contentment

"...for I have learned how to be content (satisfied to the point where I am not disturbed or disquieted) in whatever state I am."

~*PHILIPPIANS 4.11 (AMP)*

ALTHOUGH SOME OF the symptoms of depression I suffered were because of a chemical imbalance, there were times when I was just dissatisfied or discontent. In other words, I was finding everything to complain about and was not content with what I had. I'm not saying everyone who is depressed is a complainer, but it does seem to come with the territory. It is easy to see everything wrong and feel completely hopeless to change it.

The Bible tells us to be content in whatever state we are in. At one time in my life I was a stay at home mom and didn't like it at all. With my personality I am not cut out to be a at home alone. I am more of a career person at heart, so I have to practice this principle often or I will end up pretty low. It is easy to complain when life doesn't go just like you planned. When I recognized I had a habit of complaining instead of being thankful, I decided to begin developing contentment. In Philippians, Paul speaks of how he learned to be content.

"...for I have learned how to be content with whatever I have...I have learned the secret of living in every situation, whether it is with a full stomach or empty, with plenty or little" (Phil. 3.11b, 12b)

In the Greek, it suggests that contentment is a lesson learned neither in a classroom nor overnight, but through many practical experiences in life.[1] The fact that he had to learn this discipline shows us it was a process. He got to the point where he was content in every circumstance.

Contentment means getting to the point where knowing the Lord is enough. If you have nothing else in this world, you have your salvation and relationship with Jesus Christ. It is enough because you trust Him and know He is in control of every circumstance and He is with you in everything.

Remembering it is a process helps. It means there is a starting point, and as long as you continue you will reach your destination or the desired results. It is a change in our mindset. It is an attitude shift from ingratitude to gratefulness, from entitlement to gratitude. Being content is difficult when bills are not getting paid and things seem to be falling apart, but thanking God for what you do have is important. Start by waiting on God and acknowledging His sovereignty in everything.

If you are worried, bored, uneasy, restless or discouraged today, then begin the process of contentment. Begin to thank God for all you have and confess that you can do all things through Christ because He gives you the strength to be content in every situation (Phil. 4.13).

Prayer: Thank You for all that You have done for me, Lord. Forgive me for practicing the habit of complaining or ingratitude. I know you will meet all of my needs as I trust in You.

———◆———

Affirmation
I can do all things through Christ who strengthens me. I am neither discouraged nor worried. I am content in every state and put my hope in God.

———◆———

Scriptures to meditate on:

"Yet true godliness with contentment is itself great wealth. So if we have enough food and clothing, let us be content." (I Tim. 6.8)

"Don't love money; be satisfied with what you have." (Heb. 13.5a)

"Yea, doubtless, and I count all things but loss for the excellency of the knowledge of Christ Jesus my Lord: for whom I have suffered the loss of all things, and do count them but dung, that I may win Christ. That I may know him, and the power of his resurrection and the fellowship of his suffering being made conformable unto his death" (Phil. 3.8, 10).

"Do everything without complaining or arguing" (Phil. 2.14).

[1]The King James Study Bible for Women, 2003, Thomas Nelson, Inc., p. 1857

My Refuge

"I love you, LORD; you are my strength. The LORD is my rock, my fortress, and my savior; my God is my rock, in whom I find protection. He is my shield, the power that saves me, and my place of safety. I called on the LORD, who is worthy of praise, and he saved me from my enemies."

~PSALMS 18.1-3

JESUS IS A safe place to run to.

"The name of the Lord is a strong fortress; the godly run to him and are safe" *(Prov. 18.10).*

How do you run to God for a refuge? Psalms 91 verse 2 says we can declare that the Lord He is our refuge and fortress. When we are surrounded by the enemy and our hearts are full of fear, we need to say that God is our refuge and find peace in Him. We need to think on the goodness of God and receive His peace.

When I am full of fear and anxiety, I think on the name of the Lord, His character.

"And he will be called Wonderful, Counselor, the Mighty God, the Everlasting Father, the Prince of Peace" *(Isa. 9.6).*

I think about the names of Jesus in this verse. I think on the names of God and who He is to me and I find refuge and feel protected. No matter where I am I can softly sing songs about the name of Jesus, songs of deliverance.

Sometimes I would find myself in dangerous places or situations, especially when driving. One night during a psychotic episode, I was driving home from church with my children and couldn't find my way home. I drove around for a long time before I finally did. This was before we had a cell phone and I was so disoriented that everything looked unfamiliar. It was terrifying for me and my children. I still don't remember how I got home. I thank God that He protected us during those times and kept us safe. I know His angels were all around us. He is there to protect you, too. Wherever you go, He is your refuge and safety.

"For you are my hiding place; you protect me from trouble; you surround me with songs of victory" (Ps. 32.7).

Just imagine yourself surrounded by a high fortress that the enemy cannot penetrate. For me singing was my way of finding that hiding place. It helped me focus on the fact that I was surrounded by the angels of God. Songs of victory were usually songs I made up or songs declaring my freedom and liberty. Singing to the Lord helped me focus on who God is rather than the turmoil of emotions I was feeling. There were times when just finding a quiet place to sit and think on the Lord allowed me to get away and find that secret place in God. It didn't take long, just a few minutes to focus my thoughts rather than letting them run wild. It takes effort, but with practice you can learn how to focus your thoughts and bring them into the obedience of Jesus Christ. Learning how to do this is well worth the effort because it can get you through many emotional storms.

I have to say there were times when I wasn't on medication or was switching medications that I could not focus at all. My mind would race and I found it difficult to control where my thoughts went. Staying on medication was very important for me in that respect. Instrumental music often helps me during those times, as well. No singing because it might distract me even more. When the music involved singing, then I would just listen to the worship that could somehow convey what I was feeling.

One day I was sitting quietly and thinking I was taking up too much of God's time with all my needs, I heard the Lord speak to my heart that He always had time for me, because there was a place in His heart that only I could fill. Just like there is a place where only He can fill. What amazing love He has for us!

God has a secret place for you. It is the rest of the Lord where you are protected and delivered from the storms of life.

"So let us do our best to enter that rest" (Heb. 4.11).

The rest of the Lord is a place of contentment and peace. It is a place of assurance that everything will be alright.

Jesus is a safe place to run to. Run to Him today.

Prayer: Lord, You are my hiding place. I run to You for protection knowing that You are my shield from the storm. I trust in You and thank you for my freedom and liberty. Thank You for the victory over my enemies.

———◆———

Affirmation
The Lord is my refuge and my fortress. I am safe and protected.

———◆———

Scriptures to meditate on:

"Then I pray to you, O LORD. I say, "You are my place of refuge. You are all I really want in life" (Ps. 142.5).

"The LORD is a shelter for the oppressed, a refuge in times of trouble" (Ps. 9.9).

"My God is my rock, in whom I find protection. He is my shield, the power that saves me, and my place of safety. He is my refuge, my savior, the one who saves me from violence. I called on the LORD, who is worthy of praise, and he saved me from my enemies" (2 Sam. 22.3,4)

"God is our refuge and strength, always ready to help in times of trouble" (Ps. 46.1).

No Fear

"Such love has no fear, because perfect love expels all fear. If we are afraid, it is for fear of punishment, and this shows that we have not fully experienced perfect love".

~1 John 4.18

THERE IS NO fear in love. Fear paralyses while love causes you to take act. Fear disables while love enables. So to combat fear and walk in faith you have to walk in love.

What does this mean? Unforgiveness, anger, hatred, offense, resentments, and bitterness are all at the root of feelings of fear. All these emotions may even be turned toward ourselves. They torment and make us feel as though we are not good enough to receive God's love and allow it to be perfected in us.

Walking in love, without fear, is also a process. So is walking in forgiveness. It is a perfecting or maturing process. It is not something that happens overnight. It is something that takes practice and it gets better over time.

When your love for God is your motive, then you will obey Him no matter what. That's where the fearlessness comes in. As our love for Him is perfected our fear of others diminishes. People ask why Tony and I adopted our sons even though I had Bipolar and I can only come up with one answer, because God asked us to and, of course, Matthew 25, the scripture He gave our whole family about it being Him we brought into our home, was our motivation. It was bigger than our fears, even though we were fearful.

He who fears has not been made perfect in love. Living fearlessly means knowing God loves you, receiving His love, then expressing it toward others.

"But whoever keeps his word, truly the love of God is perfected in him. (1 John 2.5).

So obeying God's word perfects His love in us.

How do we perfect His love? For years I lived in fear of God's judgment as if I were a sinner rather than His child. I lived in torment and fear of God's rejection of me when I stood before Him on that Day. There were times when I lived under the delusion that I had been left behind and that I was experiencing the wrath of God where there was no hope of redemption. I didn't realize that God accepted me through His Son and that I would not be judged as a sinner but rewarded as a saint, saved by grace. Because of Christ and His love I have boldness in that Day. When I stand before Him on that day I can boldly say, "I am Yours only because of the Blood of the Lamb."

Although the delusion I was under was an indication that something was going wrong in my brain, the root of it was my perception of God. I didn't feel worthy of His love. In order to allow God's love to be perfected in me I had to first change my erroneous perception of God. I needed to see Him as my loving, Heavenly Father, not as a mean, merciless tyrant who was waiting to condemn me. As my perception of God changed into what His word said about Him, the fear began to dissolve. His love was perfected as I grew to know His love for me and it was also perfected as I obeyed His commands. It is not enough for us to just know that God loves us. We must reciprocate His love through obedience.

Are you living in fear of God? Are you living in fear? Perfect love displaces fear. Allow God to perfect His love in you.

"For we know how dearly God loves us, because he has given us the Holy Spirit to fill our hearts with his love" (Rom. 5.5).

If you are born again, the Holy Spirit fills your heart with the love of God. Get a true picture of God in your heart and mind. He's not angry with you and waiting to strike, He loves you and wants to deliver you from fear. Trust His love and character today.

Prayer: Lord Jesus, perfect Your love in me. I ask forgiveness for all bitterness or malice in my heart. Fill my heart with Your love. Help me to experience it in full measure so that I may express it to others. I know You have not given me the spirit of fear, but the spirit of love, the spirit of power and the spirit of a sound mind. I walk in faith and love today.

———————

Affirmation
Perfect love casts out fear.
There is no fear in love.
I walk in love today.

———————

Scriptures to meditate on:

"God has not given us the spirit of fear and timidity, but of power, love and self-discipline" (2 Tim. 1.7).

"I am leaving you with a gift — peace of mind and heart. And the peace I give is a gift the world cannot give. So don't be troubled or afraid" (John 14.27).

"For you have not received a spirit that makes you fearful slaves. Instead, you received God's Spirit when he adopted you as his own children. Now we call him, "Abba, Father"" (Rom. 8.15).

"And this is real love — not that we loved God, but that he loved us and sent his Son as a sacrifice to take away our sins" (1 John 4.10).

Love Walk

"What is important is faith expressing itself in love."

~GALATIANS 5.6

You CAN ALWAYS know someone's level of faith by the demonstration of their love. I can't say that I am walking in faith and not walk in love.

When I'm depressed there's sometimes an undercurrent of irritability. This irritability can take its toll on my closest relationships. As a matter of fact it was nothing for me to spend hours in prayer, go to church and then come home and be irritable and angry with everyone. Adrenalin (the spiritual high) may have played a huge part in this, too. But, how could I say that I was a woman of faith when I wasn't walking in love?

> *"...and if I had such faith that I could move mountains, but didn't love others, I would be nothing." (I Cor. 13.2c).*

Faith means nothing without love. Anger chokes out God's word in our heart.

> *"Human anger does not produce the righteousness God desires" (Jas. 1.20).*
> *"Actually, we should be slow to speak and slow to anger" (Jas. 1.19).*
> *"Love is not easily angry and is not irritable" (I Cor. 13.5).*

At this point, many people may say, "I can't help it. It is hard for me to control." God does understand and He does love us even with our faults and has given us the power through the Holy Spirit to walk in love. If your anger is due to some sort of trauma, He can heal you and bring wholeness to your life when you ask Him. We can't do this in our own power or efforts. Jesus wants us to take responsibility for our actions so that we, by the grace of God, can become more like Him.

Because of the illness and my background as a child, I thought irritability and anger was normal for me, just part of my personality. I didn't recognize that I was used to living in an angry environment and thought it was normal. Part of my anger was my environment and part of it was the illness. So I needed to walk in wisdom, which involved talking to a doctor about my anger and do what I could physically to bring my body's brain chemistry back into balance. It's hard to listen to the still, small voice of love when there are physiological issues going on.

Overcoming anger involved the right medication and the power of God's love. This was a huge opportunity for me to exercise the fruit of self-control. Taking a pill did not solve everything. It was only part of the puzzle. I needed to cooperate with the Holy Spirit as well. He has given us so much power to overcome and He expects us to recognize that we need His help.

I try to develop that self-control by thinking before I speak. Sometimes I won't say anything. Sometimes I will even have to remove myself from the situation to calm down and not say something I will regret. There were many days when I would go to God in tears about my anger and irritability towards my kids or husband. Each day I had to learn what wore me down and be aware of when I was susceptible to anger. I had to take a break from the kids and my husband and get alone with God to get an attitude adjustment. Tony would literally send me to a "time out" where I was in my room until I had gotten it together, especially if I was stressing out about something. I practice my own time out after church when I've been on a spiritual high. I think some preachers don't realize that coming down from that spiritual high from preaching may cause some irritability and anger at home. Taking a "time out" after getting home from church, as a practice, helps me to slowly adjust to being home and facing some of the responsibilities I have. I have also learned to recognize my limitations. Everyone in the house knows when I am physically and emotionally drained.

It's not easy. It is often a juggling act. There may be times when we can't help ourselves. But, God's love has been given to us and fills our hearts by the Holy Spirit (Romans 5.5). His wisdom is available to us liberally, when we ask, to help us live skillfully and avoid situations where we are set up to fail, like fatigue.

Forgiveness is an act of love and is the key to many anger issues. Displaced aggression towards your kids because you haven't forgiven your wife can be avoided when we face the person who hurt us in some way. We have to forgive quickly and forgive often in order to walk in love and peace with those around us. We also have to humbly ask forgiveness of those we hurt. I find that forgiveness doesn't just help, but it resolves many of my tendencies to act in anger. Those who have been forgiven the most, love the most.

So how is your love walk? Is there anger in your life, even wrath? Is it affecting your closest relationships? Cultivate the fruit of temperance, keep your body in balance and rested, and walk in God's power and grace daily.

Prayer: Lord, I know that anger doesn't please You. Please help me to exercise Your power and grace to love others as You love me. Thank You for filling my heart with love by Your Holy Spirit. Forgive me and heal all my broken relationships. In Jesus' name, Amen

———◆———

Affirmation
God's love fills my heart. I walk in faith
and love. I walk in the spirit of love.

———◆———

Scriptures to meditate on:

"Remembering without ceasing your work of faith, and labor of love, and patience of hope in our Lord Jesus Christ, in the sight of God and our Father." (I Thess. 1.3)

"And this is his commandment. We must believe in the name of his Son, Jesus Christ, and love one another, just as he commanded us" (I John 3.23).

"Your love for one another will prove to the world that you are my disciples" (John 13.35)

"Owe nothing to anyone — except for your obligation to love one another. If you love your neighbor, you will fulfill the requirements of God's law. Love does no wrong to others, so love fulfills the requirement of God's law" (Rom. 13.8, 10).

Crucified With Christ

"My old self has been crucified with Christ. It is no longer I who live, but Christ lives in me. So I live in this earthly body by trusting in the Son of God, who loved me and gave himself for me. I do not treat the grace of God as meaningless. For if by keeping the law could make us right with God, then there was no need for Christ to die."

~GALATIANS. 2.20,21

IT IS EASY for us to forget the price Christ paid for us. We forget that the cross is our identity. Our old self has been crucified with Christ. Our identity is in the cross and grace, not in the law and works.

So many people who live with mental illness think that the illness is their identity. You are so much more than the illness you suffer from. You are so much more than the depression. Your identity is with Christ and the cross. You are a new creation in Christ. Regardless of your behavior, your identity is in Christ. Does this mean we totally disregard our behavior and try not to be Christ-like? Not at all! Instead, we allow the Holy Spirit to do the work in us to make the changes inside us that reflect Christ more and more. We don't belong to God because of what we do, it is what Christ has done that makes us who we are.

For years I identified with condemnation and shame because of the abuse I suffered as a child. I felt guilty about everything and was constantly battling false guilt. I felt guilty whether I did something wrong or not. Consequently, I was always trying to find a way to work and make things right. I tried to make myself right with God through what I did and following all the rules. It was legalism and religion rather than faith in Christ and His grace. Although I grew up in the church, I didn't hear much about the grace of God. I grew up in a very legalistic denomination and legalism was all I knew. I had to unlearn my legalistic perception of God and my relationship with Him and learn how to walk in His grace through faith. Talk about crucifixion. Everything I knew before had to die.

One of the symptoms of Bipolar and depression is self-loathing. It is a feeling of not being able to do anything right and of tremendous guilt when you can't. I would confess and confess and confess my sins and still feel guilty that I had to do something to make it right, so I would spend hours in prayer. It became compulsive. I would do something wrong and up to my room I would go to do my penance. It got to the point where Tony really didn't want me to spend more than so much time in my room in prayer, which was actually more like doing penance. To me, it was all about performance. It was based mostly on what other people thought of me. And I didn't think God thought much of me outside my performance of works.

You cannot live by faith and works. You have to believe and trust in the work that was done at the cross and walk in the grace that has been freely given or trust in your own efforts.

"For it is by grace you are saved through faith, it is a gift from God and not based on our good works" (Eph. 2.8).

There is nothing we can do to make ourselves right with God. Jesus is the only one who can make us righteous and we can stand secure in Him.

When I depended on works to make me right with God, I was treating the grace of God as meaningless. I frustrated the grace of God and had actually fallen from grace (Gal. 5.4). That is a dangerous place to be because without grace, we stand before God on our righteousness rather than Christ's. Basically, our works will never be enough.

The cross defeated the devil. So every time he brought accusations against me, I would sing this verse in Galatians. I am crucified with Christ. That became my identity. That was my weapon, my faith in the cross.

In the military (I'm a military brat and wife) we were given I.D. cards which gave us access to certain privileges. The I.D. card had a picture and my name. I didn't have to work a day for the Government, I was given one just because of my relationship to my dad and my husband. I was their dependent.

That is how it works with our identity in Christ. Through Christ's sacrifice, He has given us an I.D. card that has been purchased by His blood. He did and does all the work, but it is our picture and name on the card. Our identity is in Him. There is no use in trying to work for access to His forgiveness, grace, acceptance and righteousness. All we have to do is become His dependent by receiving His grace through faith in His death at Calvary.

"So now there is no condemnation for those who belong to Christ Jesus." (Rom. 8.1)

If you deal with guilt today, then you need to know that as a child of God there is no condemnation in Christ.

"God sent his Son into the world not to judge the world, but to save the world through him" (John 3.17).

I always wondered why Jesus kept the wounds in His hands, feet and side. Why didn't He just heal them along with His resurrection? He could have made the evidence of His wounds disappear, but He kept them. I believe it is a reminder. Why would He want to remember that pain? Maybe to let us forever know that He identifies with our pain and to show us that our wounds are our glory. That because of our wounds, we can identify with the pain of others and we can identify with His wounds.

"I am crucified with Christ; it is no longer I who live, but it is Christ who lives in me; and the life I now live I live in the flesh I live by faith in the Son of God who loved me and gave himself for me" (Gal. 2.20).

Jesus never came to condemn. When you do something wrong, be quick to admit it and say, "I'm so sorry, Jesus" and get it right. The hard part is not allowing the devil to put guilt on you. Resist the temptation to "make up for it" and do penance, unless the Lord specifically tells you to do something like asking forgiveness from someone you've hurt.

"But if we confess our sins to him, he is faithful and just to forgive us our sins and to cleanse us from all wickedness" (I John 1.9).

It is an act of faith to ask the Lord to forgive you and then, by faith trust that He has cleansed you from that sin. Because of His sacrifice, not our penance or by how we feel.

You are crucified with Christ and live by faith in the One who loved you and gave Himself for you. Resist the guilt and put on Christ Jesus. Resist the devil and don't listen to his accusations. When those thoughts come, show your I.D. which is to say, identify yourself with Christ. You are His dependent and He will claim you every time.

Prayer: Thank You, Jesus, for my Heavenly I.D. card. and that I am crucified with Christ. Help me to live by faith in Your Son and not in my works or abilities. Deliver me from legalism and religion. I enter into Your grace and walk by faith in the Son of God. Thank You for claiming me as Yours and for Your love for me.

————◆————

Affirmation
I will walk in the grace of God. I am free
from works and will not be entangled by them.

————◆————

Scriptures to meditate on:

"So Christ has truly set us free. Now make sure that you stay free, and don't get tied up again in slavery to the law" (Gal. 5.1).

"*Therefore, since we have been made right in God's sight by faith, we have peace with God because of what Jesus Christ has done for us. Because of our faith, Christ has brought us into this place of undeserved privilege where we now stand, and we confidently and joyfully look forward to sharing God's glory. For the sin of this one man, Adam, caused death to rule over many. But even greater is God's wonderful grace and his gift of righteousness for all who receive it will live in triumph over sin and death through this one man, Jesus Christ. God's law was given so that all people could see how sinful they were. But as people sinned more and more, God's wonderful grace became more abundant*" (Rom. 5.1,2,17, 20)

"*Sin is no longer your master, for you no longer live under the requirements of the law. Instead, you live under the freedom of God's grace*" (Rom. 6.14).

Justified

"Therefore, since we have been made right in God's sight by faith, we have peace with God because of what Jesus Christ our Lord has done for us"

~ROMANS 5.1

THE FEELINGS OF false guilt, that nagging feeling that you've done something wrong when you haven't, were caused by my thinking that I was never in right standing with God. I had no peace and was full of anxiety. I felt rejected by God and not acceptable to Him no matter what I did. It became a habitual cycle of doing penance until I "felt" right, then after doing something wrong, doing penance again, which needed to be broken. It became an obsessive compulsive attempt to wash myself spiritually when I was already clean. It's sad, because it is almost as if I were self- mutilating to get the sin out, or washing my hands fifty times a day just to show how sorry I was for what I did.

My favorite shows are courtroom dramas like Matlock and Perry Mason. I like these shows because the innocent is always vindicated and the guilty person is caught. I think the courtroom is a picture of what goes on in Heaven every day. There is the devil who is always accusing us day and night.

"For the accuser of our brothers and sisters has been thrown down to the earth — the one who accuses them before our God day and night" (Rev. 12.10).

There is God who is the Righteous Judge;

"…You have come to God Himself, who is the judge over all things" (Heb. 12.23).

Then, there is Jesus, who is the defense attorney, our Advocate;

"But if anyone does sin, we have an advocate who pleads our case before the Father. He is Jesus Christ, the one who is truly righteous" (1 John 2.1).

We stand as the accused.

The enemy is constantly accusing us to God and to ourselves. Then, he turns around and makes accusations about God to us. He does this to take away the peace we have with God through Christ, but Jesus justifies us. Not because we always do right, but because of what He did at the cross. He took our place as guilty even though He was innocent, thus, we are found "Not guilty" when we stand before God. We are made righteous or put in right standing with God because of His blood and because He died for our sins. In other words, since Christ stood in our place as the accused, we can stand before God, in the courtroom of Heaven, as the righteous or innocent.

"He is so rich in kindness and grace that he purchased our freedom with the blood of his Son and forgave our sins" (Eph. 1.7).

Jesus paid the penalty. He redeemed or bought us back from hell and sin.

When I read the above scripture in Romans, I realized I had peace with God and that I didn't have to feel guilty any longer. When I felt that guilt, I believed I had peace with God; not because of how I felt, but because it was true. My confidence in His acceptance of me grows more and more as I pray to God, thanking Him for the blood of Jesus which paid for the sin I commit. I have to believe it. Not because I feel it, but because it is true.

So many times when we are feeling guilty, we stop praying or approaching God our Father. That is what the enemy wants us to do. He wants us to begin to withdraw from God or try to approach Him only when we "feel" right. During times of depression you can often feel empty and far from God, but Jesus died to give us access to the throne of God. He died so we can have fellowship with the Father.

"So let us come boldly before His throne of our gracious God" (Heb. 4.16).

So stop seeing yourself as the accused or always "Guilty as Charged" without hope. See yourself as righteous. You are innocent until proven guilty and Jesus took all the proof and nailed it to the cross, defeating Satan. He has no power over you.

"He cancelled the record of the charges against us and took it away by nailing it to the cross" (Col. 2.14).

God sees you as innocent and has thrown the case out. He sees you through the blood of Jesus, and Jesus, your Advocate, declares you righteous. It is good enough. Now walk in peace with God and the peace that is from God.

Prayer: Father, thank You that I am righteous before you today. Thank You for the blood of Jesus that justifies me and makes me righteous before You. I receive Your peace today, in Jesus' name, Amen.

———◆———

Affirmation
I am the righteous because of Christ Jesus.
I am justified and have peace with God.

———◆———

Scriptures to meditate on:

"For God presented Jesus as the sacrifice for sin. People are made right with God when they believe that Jesus sacrificed his life, shedding his blood" (Rom. 3.25)

"...our acquittal is not based on obeying the law. It is based on faith. So we are made right with God through faith and not by obeying the law" (Rom. 3.27b-28).

"And this righteousness will bring peace. Yes, it will bring quietness and confidence forever" (Is. 32.17).

"To the praise of the glory of his grace, wherein he hath made us accepted in the beloved" (Eph. 1.6).

"For God presented Jesus as the sacrifice for sin. People are made right with God when they believe that Jesus sacrificed His life, shedding His blood" (Rom. 3.25).

"...our acquittal is not based on obeying the Law. It is based on faith. So we are made right with God through faith and not by obeying the law" (Rom. 3.27b, 28).

No Shame

"Instead of shame and dishonor, you will enjoy a double share of honor"

~ISAIAH 61.7

THERE IS A stigma associated with any form of mental illness that tends to bring shame. Whether it is Bipolar, Schizophrenia, Depression, ADHD or something else, society has placed a stigma around people who struggle with mental illness. The media portrays mental illness as evil and violent because many of the mass shootings have in some way been connected to mental illness. The myth is that if you were strong enough or good enough you wouldn't have to deal with this. In the church, the idea is that there must be some type of sin in your life that is causing you to suffer. In other countries it is believed that it is because of demons and evil spirits. It's like the Hunchback of Notre Dame. There is such a fear of what we don't understand that we miss out on someone who has worth and value. We would prefer to keep the mentally ill out of sight and out of mind, like Quasimodo living in a bell tower.

For years I was ashamed to even admit I needed medication to function. I would think, "If only I was strong enough, I wouldn't need medication." Then, when I didn't take it I had to deal with the shame of hospitalizations, psychotic episodes and bizarre behavior that my family had to endure. At times, the side effects were worse than the disease. Then, I found this scripture:

"Instead of shame and dishonor, you will enjoy a double share of honor" (Is. 61.7).

God does bring you double honor. A few years ago, we adopted two little boys, two toddlers. We already had three teenage daughters and now have five children. In my eyes, it was double honor to be their mother, but with it brought the risk of disgrace. Caseworkers had told us during training that people who had Bipolar should never be parents; there was a huge chance of relapsing. The stress of adjusting to this huge change almost caused me to have a relapse, but through the grace of God, He helped me, along with my husband, Tony to raise five children who love the Lord and who give me double honor.

It doesn't mean I go through life without any regard to my behavior or without any regard to others. It means I do not let the feelings of shame hold me back from achieving what God has for my life and for my family.

The definition of shame is "a painful emotion caused by a strong sense of guilt, embarrassment, unworthiness or disgrace." I think the key word here is guilt. The devil loves to keep us tied to some painful event in our past. Those who are associated with someone who struggles with mental illness may experience some shame, too.

Another definition of shame is the statements we tell ourselves: "I'm not good enough," and, "Who do you think you are?" I thought because I struggled with mental illness, I was disqualified to do anything for God or of anything of significance. People may try to disqualify us, but God doesn't. He never sees us as defective. He sees us as vessels with treasures He deposits into to benefit others. People may see our disease, but the fruit in our lives should speak for itself. Am I good enough in and of myself? No. It's Christ. Can the fruit of goodness be demonstrated in my life? Yes, through Christ. We are nothing without Him.

Believe it or not, Jesus can relate. He became sin for us. We run this race by, "… keeping our eyes on Jesus, the champion who initiates and perfects our faith. Because of the joy awaiting him, he endured the cross, disregarding its shame. Now he is seated in the place of honor beside God's throne" (Heb. 12.3).

Jesus is the perfect example of working through shame to obey God and then receiving double honor. He is seated at the right hand of the throne of God. Jesus hung on the cross in open shame, yet He was innocent. It looked like defeat, yet He was victorious. He looked past the shame to the joy ahead and believed God's promises.

A relapse or an episode may bring great shame and we are tempted to just give up our race and quit. It is tempting to think there's no point in getting up and pushing past what looks like defeat, but despite what it looks like, we are seated in those heavenly places with Christ and are victorious with Him.

You do not have this affliction because you are a weak person or because there is sin in your life. The disciples thought this about a blind man, but Jesus answered: "It was not because of his sins or his parents' sins," ... "This happened so the power of God could be seen in him" (John 9.3).

The devil would like you to live your life full of shame and never move forward to obey God. He would love for you to draw back and withdraw from life. His goal is to keep us from God's plan. Our goal is to glorify God by fulfilling it. God wants you to know He has a purpose and plan for your life. He doesn't want you to live in shame and has promised double honor if you continue to live right before Him and obey Him no matter the cost.

God has promised us double honor for your shame.

Prayer: Father, thank You for Your promises. Thank You that You will give me double honor for my shame. Help me to live a life that is pleasing to You despite this affliction. That I may live a life that glorifies You in everything I say and do.

———◆———

Affirmation
God will be glorified in me as I go through this.

———◆———

Additional scriptures:

"She is clothed with strength and dignity and she laughs without fear of the future" (Prov. 31.25).

"Come back to the place of safety, all you prisoners who still have hope! I promise this very day that I will repay two blessings for each of your troubles" (Zech. 9.12).

Good Confessions

"...Speaking to yourselves in psalms and hymns and spiritual songs, singing and making melody in your heart to the Lord."

~EPHESIANS 5.19

I WAS HAVING another one of those stressful days at work wondering how I was going to make it through. I knew I was slipping away from reality and that things were not right, but if I did what I felt like doing it would not be good. So I began to sing a song under my breath while I filed. I had the toughest time of my life trying not to just give up trying. Some of you know what I mean. In order to do that, I had to be careful of what I said to others, and most of all, what I said to myself. I had to have a good confession. I had to confess the Good News of what God was saying about me rather than what I was feeling. I knew I needed positive thoughts and positive words working on my behalf going through my mind. You cannot have positive thoughts without positive words. Neither can you have positive words without positive thoughts.

Psychotic episodes are terrifying. Some don't make it through them without causing harm to themselves or others. It is also very scary for my family because sometimes I just stop talking and no one understands the thoughts behind my actions. During episodes it is difficult, if not impossible, to control where your thoughts go. It is hard for others to understand that concept. The only way I can explain it is that our flesh (our mind, will and emotions) is always hostile towards God. When we have a healthy brain, which houses our mind, we have the capacity to obey the Holy Spirit. When our brain or body is not healthy, we tend to obey the fleshly part of our thinking.

It is easy to quote the scripture that we should cast down the thoughts that argue against God when you have a healthy brain, but to will yourself to be able to do it when you are not healthy is a difficult. One of the only ways I can stand is through focusing our thoughts instead of working to cast them down. It can be overwhelming. We cannot will ourselves to think better, but we can pray to God and thank Him to make it through the temptation to give up.

My last psychotic episode, I'm sorry to say, was over an oversight of ordering my medication. It threw my brain for a loop and I was over the edge before I knew it. I knew I couldn't just allow my thoughts to torment me and run rampant, yet they did. Somehow I had to focus on Christ rather than speak all of my fear filled words to those around me. Thankfully, I work at a Christian ministry and I had co-workers who were full of the love of God, even though they didn't understand what was going on. They reminded me of the truth. Not many people are as fortunate and have people to remind themselves of the truth.

"God must be mad at me" always seems to surface, which causes me to panic even more. But, rather than just quote scripture and get frustrated when I couldn't remember anything, I would do my best to get quiet and remember God's love for me, speaking to myself. The most important thing was to remember that He was with me.

Some people think that having a good confession is like being the Little Engine that could, where if you repeat a certain scripture or words over and over, you will make it up that proverbial hill. If you believe with all your might. Confessing what God says about the situation, Him or yourself is not a way to manipulate God to make the symptoms go away or to change our situation or circumstance. It is a way to change our focus to a God who can do the impossible, who loves us always and is in complete control. It is the way we get to the point where we truly believe what we confess with our mouth about the Lord Jesus Christ. It helps us say "Yes" to Him in the midst of the worst storms. We have to hold fast to those confessions or we will be swept away by those storms.

In one instance, Tony took me to the doctor knowing I was showing symptoms of psychosis, and instead of telling her what I was really thinking and how I was really feeling, I just quoted a scripture. She looked at Tony and told him she didn't see anything wrong with me. Confession should not keep us in denial of what we need to do in the natural.

Thanking God for His love through a song (it doesn't have to be one you know. You can just make one up. always helps me.) "Yes, Jesus loves me" is a good song and confession.

It is a battle. When there is a chemical imbalance the devil loves to take advantage of our weaknesses. He loves to cause more suffering for the believer with tormenting thoughts and he is waiting for the words we speak to cause fear and doubt when we hear them. There is a difference between telling someone what is going on with you so they can pray for you and constantly saying you are a failure, like Eyore in Winnie the Pooh.

"Faith comes by hearing the Good News about Christ" (Rom. 10.17).

I think it is safe to say that fear comes by hearing bad news. It didn't seem to matter whether it came from my own words or the six o'clock news.

In Ephesians 5.8 it says we should "sing psalms, hymns and spiritual songs among yourselves and make melodies in our heart to the Lord." I made a melody in my heart to the Lord and gave thanks to Him for all things in Jesus Christ.

When we cannot think of a particular verse or scripture, then we sing a new song, a song of thanksgiving and praise and a song of worship.

"Sing a new song of praise to him…" (Ps. 33.3).
"He has given me a new song to sing, a hymn of praise to our God" (Ps. 40.3)

There is such sweet fellowship during times of suffering when we just sing because God is good. When we sing as if God is with us and that He can hear us. One thing we must remember is that the Holy Spirit will keep us. It is His job to keep us and to present us to God, and He will. When it is all said and done, it is God who does the work and fights for us. We can only do our best to keep our eyes on Him through songs and our words.

Looking back, I felt like I was playing the opposite game. My family was confused because they didn't understand that there were two things I had to resist with my words, the lie that God was mad at me, and the lie that He had abandoned me, no matter what others may say to you. No matter where your thoughts may take you, remember who God really is and remember His love and mercy. Thank Him for who He is and, sing those songs to Him.

If you know someone who is suffering from mental illness or depression speak encouraging words to them and offer to pray for them. I had a friend who would call and leave a song on my voicemail. It was just what I needed when I needed it. My mother would leave a prayer on my voicemail and just tell me she was thinking of me.

God is on your side and you are not alone. The Holy Spirit knows how to keep you. There is power in your words. There is power in your songs.

Prayer: Surround me with songs of deliverance today, Lord. Put a new song in my mouth, a song of praise, even though I may not feel like singing. I will trust in You when I am afraid. Thank You for being with me and for you Spirit who keeps me.

———◆———

Affirmation
I will sing to the Lord a new song. I worship the Lord in Spirit and in truth. I make melody in my heart to the Lord.

———◆———

Scriptures to meditate on:

"The godly will rejoice in the Lord and find shelter in him. And those who do what is right will praise him" (Ps.64.10).

"For you are my hiding place, you protect me from trouble. You surround me with songs of victory" (Ps. 32.7).

"The tongue can bring death or life..." (Prov. 18.21).

The Mind of Christ

*"... But we have the mind of Christ (the Messiah) and do hold the
thoughts (feelings and purposes) of His heart"*

~1 Corinthians 2.16, AMP

SOMETHING I TELL myself often is that I have the mind of Christ. One of the most
difficult things for me to do when I am struggling mentally is to make good decisions. It is tempting to be impulsive or to lose self-control or totally avoid any
kind of conflict with my children. So when my thought processes are not clear,
I need to remember and tell myself I have the mind of Christ.

This means I possess His thoughts, opinions, judgments, plans and emotions. It automatically means that to hurt myself or someone else is out of the
question. It means I possess His ability to understand what the Holy Spirit is
saying to me. It is not easy when you think that every voice speaking to you is
the voice of God.

I know that people have a difficult time telling someone they are having
thoughts of suicide. Suicide is not a normal function of the brain. When you are
"having thoughts of suicide" it is more than just feeling sad and wanting to take
your life. It is an indication that something in your brain, as well as your heart, is
going wrong and it needs to be tended to. Your brain is an organ just like your liv-
er and kidney and needs attention just like any other organ and medication may be
able to bring it back into balance. Also, be aware of medications that may actually
cause you to have suicidal thoughts. Depression is really a warning light to let you
know something is wrong. It may not just be spiritual causes. It could be physical.

When I had suicidal thoughts they would sound something like, I just want to go home ("home" being Heaven) or I wish I could just go to sleep and wake up in Heaven. Every night I would go to sleep and wish I woke up in Heaven, for that to happen I knew I would have to die. I wanted to escape all of the stress and all of the pain. Having the mind of Christ is knowing how much God loves you and that He has a purpose for you here on Earth, a great purpose that He wants to fulfill through you. Having the mind of Christ means He would never want you be taken away from your loved ones by your own hand and leave them. You may not see it today but each day you live you get closer to seeing God's purpose fulfilled in you. It takes perseverance and courage to wake up each day knowing you are on God's heart and mind. Perseverance is a fruit of the Spirit. You can endure until the end. Don't give in to temptation. Don't isolate yourself. Find someone you can talk to about those thoughts, especially if they persist for more than a few days.

It's hard to have the mind of Christ when your brain is not functioning well. When you are psychotic and having hallucinations or disorganized thinking, it is hard to believe you are, because everything within you says differently.

Whenever I doubted my own ability to discern God's direction, I would ask a friend. I would ask specifically if I was processing my thoughts right. In 1 Timothy 1.6 it says that God has given us the Spirit of a sound mind which means the ability to make right decisions and exercise self-discipline.

I have heard about some people with bipolar who spend outrageous amounts of money without any restraint. Some people, during a manic episode, will go out and buy a car or a house or run up their credit cards. Having the mind of Christ definitely means practicing self-control. I am susceptible to doing the same so I have set financial boundaries and consult Tony before even making minor purchases, so when I am struggling with the temptation to go on a shopping spree, I have a built in habit I don't have to think about.

If you are tempted to do something impulsive, talk to your spouse or a friend before purchasing anything or doing anything you may regret – you may not think it I "inappropriate" at the time. Wisdom says find a friend who will hold you accountable for the decisions you need to make.

Having the mind of Christ means you love what He loves and hate what He hates. It also means you have God's wisdom to help you make right decisions.

"If you need wisdom — if you want to know what God wants you to do—ask Him and he will gladly tell you. He will not resent your asking" (Jas. 1.15).

If we ask God for wisdom, He will give it to us, usually through our spouses or close friends.

Again, it means you are not to hurt yourself or anyone else. If you are pre-occupied with hurting yourself or someone else, please immediately notify a doctor or psychiatrist. If you don't have access to a doctor, pray and ask God to help you find someone to tell so you are not isolated and alone with those frightening thoughts. If you are the family member of someone who is preoccupied with going to Heaven or taking his or her life, don't take these conversations lightly and hope they will just get over it. It is imperative that you encourage them to see a doctor, a pastor, minister or therapist.

Prayer: Lord, help me to make good decisions that are based on Your love. Help me to exercise self control and to obey You in all things throughout the day. I know that Your thoughts are many concerning me and that I am on Your heart and mind today.

———◆———

Affirmation
I have the mind of Christ. I have a sound mind and make healthy, wise decisions.

———◆———

Scriptures to meditate on:

"Don't turn your back on wisdom, for she will protect you. Love her, and she will guard you. Getting wisdom is the wisest thing you can do! And whatever else you do, develop good judgment" (Prov. 4.6)

"When the Spirit of truth comes, he will guide you into all truth" (John 16.13a).

"My sheep listen to my voice; I know them, and they follow me" (John 10.27).

"For I know the plans I have for you," says the Lord. "They are plans for good and not for disaster, to give you a future and a hope" (Jer. 29.11).

"How precious are your thoughts about me, O God. They cannot be numbered" (Ps.139.17).

"And now, dear brothers and sisters, one final thing. Fix your thoughts on what is true, and honorable, and right, and pure, and lovely, and admirable. Think about things that are excellent and worthy of praise" (Phil. 4.8).

His Grace is Sufficient

"Each time he said, 'My grace is all you need.
My power works best in weakness."

~2 CORINTHIANS 12.9

A COMMON RESPONSE of most Believers to someone who suffers from any form of mental illness is they have a lack of faith, otherwise he or she would not be suffering with this type of affliction. Some say we should just believe God more. The devil is always the one who tells us we don't have enough faith. God always says, "My grace is all you need."

God's grace is more than His unmerited favor. Grace is actually His granting us the ability to do what God has called us to do. Paul needed grace to accomplish God's will and calling, even while he was suffering. When my husband and I decided to adopt, I was very fearful. I actually tried to bargain with God. "Ok, Lord. If you want me to adopt, then I want complete healing. Promise me that I will have no more episodes and it's a deal." Like Paul, I didn't think I could do what He asked me with such a debilitating limitation. I was afraid of a relapse and I was afraid it might cost me everything. I made all these excuses about why I couldn't obey God. Then, I read this scripture above and decided to take the risk and trust what Jesus told Paul. His grace is sufficient and there were no promises I would not be weak, but that His strength would be perfected when I am. Instead of adopting one child, we adopted two toddlers. I should not be able to do what I am doing, yet I am, despite my limitations.

According to First Peter, it is because of our faith, many times, that we suffer in the first place. The question is never if we have enough faith, but what kind of faith do we want? The devil is always after our faith. It is of great price. He wants us to begin to accuse God when things don't go the way we want. He wants us to turn our back on God. On those days when I didn't think I would make it, God's grace got me through one more day. God's grace got me through another hour.

We need to stop beating ourselves up when we suffer. God's grace is sufficient. We get stuck on asking God why we still suffer from these symptoms. His purpose for our suffering is revealed in the verse above. His power works best in our weakness.

Does that mean God brings the suffering? No. It means He uses it for His glory. There were many times when I felt so down and worthless and I would go to church and invariably someone would hug me or come up to me and say "You are such a blessing to me." How could I be a blessing to someone in the state I was in? It is strange, but somehow when we are at our worst, Christ still shines through our weakness. When we suffer we share in the suffering of Christ. We can learn to rejoice in the fact that there is a fellowship in the place of suffering.

That may not be easy for you to see today, but when you are on the other side, you will be able to say that God was there in the midst of everything. He is here right now through your suffering. Even when you are weak He is strong.

I used to think I was weak because I have a mental illness. I know now that there is great strength every time we go through a trial. People with strong, type A personalities are just as susceptible to having mental health issues as anyone else. It really doesn't matter. When we are depressed, it is not a question of weak faith. If it were based on your faith, then you just might be able to deliver yourself. It would be all about your faith in your faith rather than a faith in God as the Deliverer.

You have faith today. You have enough faith to believe that God's strength is made perfect in your weakness. His grace is all you need. Walk in it today.

Prayer: Thank You Lord for Your strength being perfected in my weakness. Thank You that Your grace is enough to sustain me today. I walk in Your grace one day at a time and trust that You are glorified even in my suffering.

———◆———

Affirmation
I have faith.
God's grace is sufficient for me.

———◆———

Scriptures to meditate on:

"Dear friends, don't be surprised at the fiery trials you are going through as if something strange were happening to you. Instead, be very glad — for these trials make you partners with Christ in his suffering, so that you will have the wonderful joy of seeing his glory when it is revealed to all the world" (1 Pet. 4.12, 13).

"I want to know Christ and experience the mighty power that raised him from the dead. I want to suffer with him, sharing in his death" (Phil. 3.10).

"So be truly glad. There is wonderful joy ahead, even though you have to endure many trials for a little while. These trials will show that your faith is genuine. It is being tested as fire tests and purifies gold — though your faith is far more precious than mere gold" (I Pet. 1.7).

He Rejoices Over Me

"He will take delight in you with gladness. With his love, he will calm all your fears. He will rejoice over you with joyful songs."

~*Zephaniah. 3.17*

ONE OF THE symptoms of bipolar or depression is feelings of worthlessness. Thoughts that may start with, "Why do I even bother", or "I can't seem to do anything right." There were days when I felt like I should just stay in bed and not even try to do anything. Then there were days when I did make it out of bed and everything seemed to go wrong. Nothing seemed to work out right. At the end of the day, I would feel like a complete failure.

It is easy to think sometimes God feels the same about us. We begin to think and believe that God is very disappointed with us and ready to throw His hands up and walk away. That could not be further from the truth.

I was having one of those days where I was beating myself up and thinking, "What a mess I am and what a mess I have made of this day." I was at work and making mistakes and not feeling very good about myself. I just let out one big, long sigh. In that sigh held all of my emotions and feelings about the day, that it was a total loss, but it was as if the Lord heard all the longing and disappointment and gave me a picture of Him dancing and singing on a mountain. How could He rejoice over me when things were going downhill?

I believe the Lord gave me a picture of this verse to assure me that when I feel like a failure, He doesn't lose heart. He is not at a loss, but is rejoicing over me. He was rejoicing because He saw my future. It had an expected end (Jeremiah 29.11), He was in control and I was not a failure, but an overcomer and more than a conqueror (Rom. 8.37).

"He will rest [in silent satisfaction] and in His love He will be silent and make no mention [of past sins, or even recall them]" (Zeph. 3.a7, AMP).

As far as Jesus is concerned, our future with Him is a done deal. There is no doubt in His mind. He is the potter we are the clay. He already has in mind the end result and we are in good hands. Jesus is the Author and Completer of our faith. He rejoices over us because He sees the finished product. Once this day is over and I confess everything to Him, He has already put the day behind Him, along with all my mistakes and failures. It's a new day.

Now if He rejoices over you, you can rejoice with Him. You can rejoice that things will not always be the same. You will not always be depressed. God is not finished with you, yet. You can especially rejoice when things look their worst. Get a picture of Him dancing and singing songs of joy over you. He is humming over the potter's wheel. If He has begun a work in you, He will complete it. (Phil. 1.6).

Before going to bed tonight write down all the things you think you have done wrong at work or at home. Tell God all about them, then thank Him for forgetting them. Throw the paper in the trash and do a little dance. Regardless of how you are feeling, know that God is not disappointed in you. He is rejoicing over you and singing songs of joy at the finished work. Picture the Master Carpenter whistling as He works and remember, IT'S A DONE DEAL.

Prayer: Father, Thank You for Your Love for me. Thank You for watching over the work that You are doing in my life. I trust You will complete it to Your satisfaction.

———•———

Affirmation
God rejoices over me with singing and songs of joy.
He will perfect that which concerns me.

———•———

Scriptures to meditate on:

"Those who have been ransomed by the LORD will return. They will enter Jerusalem singing, crowned with everlasting joy. Sorrow and mourning will disappear, and they will be filled with joy and gladness" (Is. 35.10)

"You have turned my mourning into joyful dancing. You have taken away my clothes of mourning and clothed me with joy" (Ps. 30.11).

"Then the Lord gave me this message. "O Israel, can I not do to you as this potter has done to his clay? As the clay is in the potter's hand, so are you in my hand" (Jer. 18.5, 6).

Complete in Him

"So you are complete through your union with Christ..."

~COLOSSIANS 2.10

THERE ARE TIMES when I ask, "Will my healing ever be complete?" When my thoughts go down that road, I recognize that I am complete in Christ. Even though I may not see the completion of my healing, I know I am complete in Christ and that is how my Heavenly Father sees me.

Being "complete" means I have been filled with Him and that I have every spiritual blessing residing in me and in Heaven.

"All praise to God, the Father of our Lord Jesus Christ, who has blessed us with every spiritual blessing in the heavenly realms because we are united with Christ"(Eph. 1.3).

It's easy to believe this when everything in your life is going well and you are not dealing with any afflictions, but when you are faced with affliction or infirmity, it is important that you believe what God says about you regardless of what you see. It is important to know you have every spiritual blessing inside you and that your healing is being done from the inside out. Your outside just hasn't caught up with your inside yet. You are a new creation.

Colossians continues to explain the spiritual blessings that we have:

When you came to Christ, you were "circumcised," but not by a physical procedure. Christ performed a spiritual circumcision — the cutting away of your sinful nature. For you were buried with Christ when you were baptized. And with him you were raised to new life because you trusted the might power of God, who raised Christ from the dead. You were dead because of your sins and because your sinful nature was not yet cut away. Then God made you alive with Christ, for he forgave all your sins. He canceled the record of the charges against us and took it away by nailing it to the cross. In this way, he disarmed the spiritual rulers and authorities. He shamed them publicly by his victory over them on the cross. (Col. 2.11-15)

One is we are raised from our old life, 2) we have new life in Christ, 3) the curse of the law has been removed, and 4) Satan and all demonic forces have been conquered. Focusing on what I have in Christ helps me to know that I have everything I need to handle the challenges of life.

This is one of my favorite scriptures because I felt I was broken and that my life was just one giant, incomplete puzzle. Every day was so unpredictable. I never knew what I would face from day to day or week to week, but Jesus began to put the pieces of my broken life together day by day. Through every trial I grow stronger and closer to Him.

Completion also means spiritual maturity. There are things we obtain through trials of the flesh that we don't procure any other way. Our character is being developed through tribulation.

Because of our faith, Christ has brought us into this place of undeserved privilege where we now stand, and we confidently and joyfully look forward to sharing God's glory. We can rejoice, too, when we run into problems and trials, for we know that they help us develop endurance. And endurance develops strength of character, and character strengthens our confident hope of salvation. And this hope will not lead to disappointment. For we know how dearly God loves us, because he has given us the Holy Spirit to fill our hearts with his love (Rom, 5.2-5).

With every challenge and trial I should be growing in Christ-like character. I should be gaining more strength, more hope, more love, and more peace with every struggle until my outside is as whole as my inside and I look like Him.

Asking why I still have not received my complete healing or why I still have symptoms is the wrong question. It is the wrong thing to focus on. When I experience symptoms, I begin thanking God for my wholeness. I was healed at Calvary, I am being healed today, and I will be completely healed at His return. He is the One who was, and is, and is to come. When we get so focused on results, we don't appreciate the process.

You are complete in Him today. You have everything you need to make it through the day. Be aware of the present, of right now. You are complete right now regardless of what you are experiencing. If Jesus Christ is the Lord of your life, then you are filled with Him. Your faith in God's word is what brings wholeness.

Prayer: Thank You that I am complete in You, Lord. Help me realize and recognize all of the blessings that You have blessed me with. In Your name, Amen.

———•———

Affirmation
*I have all spiritual blessings residing in me and in Heaven. I am a new creature, redeemed from the curse, I have a new life,
I have authority over the enemy.*

———•———

Scriptures to meditate on:

"Can anything ever separate us from Christ's love? Does it mean he no longer loves us if we have trouble or calamity, or are persecuted, or hungry or destitute, or in danger, or threatened with death? No, despite all these things, overwhelming victory is ours through Christ, who loved us" (Rom. 8.35, 37).

"But thank God! He gives us victory over sin and death through our Lord Jesus Christ" (1 Cor. 15.57).

"But thank God! He has made us his captives and continues to lead us along in Christ's triumphal procession. Now he uses us to spread the knowledge of Christ everywhere, like a sweet perfume" (2 Cor. 2.14).

"All praise to God the Father of our Lord Jesus Christ, who has blessed us with every spiritual blessing in the heavenly realms because we are united with Christ" (Eph. 1.3).

He is Faithful

"True, some of them were unfaithful; but just because they were un-faithful, does that mean God will be unfaithful? Of course not! Even if everyone else is a liar, God is true".

~ROMANS. 3.3, 4A

GOD IS FAITHFUL even when we are not.

I have a hard time finishing things. I have so many projects half way done, it's ridiculous. But God always finishes what He starts. He always sees it through to the end.

There are days when I feel like an unfinished project. I feel like I am just constantly working on one thing or another and I wonder if it will ever be done. As we said before, we are complete in Him and full of Him. We are also a work in progress. We are God's workmanship, created to bring Him glory. The fact that God is faithful gives me so much hope when I am not faithful. When I fall short and don't follow through I can trust that God will never give up on me. He will keep working on me until Jesus returns.

For years it seemed like I continually went around the same mountain over and over again. I thought, "Why am I here again?" Being committed to mental hospitals seemed to be the lowest points of my life, especially when it kept happening over and over again. For it to happen once, most people could understand. But for it to have happened often, most people would just give up and walk away. I felt so alone and as if God would give up on me like others had. I thought that all the hospitalizations disqualified me for service or ministry. I used to think that being on medication disqualified me, but God never disqualified me. Through it all He would minister to me and lovingly raise me up again. He blessed my family, too. I am thankful to have a husband who would not walk away.

My daughter and I were talking one day and she was telling me that she felt like she was going around the same mountain over and over. I told her that after every trip around that mountain we get stronger because the enemy wants you to give up on yourself and on God. Instead, our faith gets stronger each time we get back up. The devil always takes us around just one time too many. I told her that it's that one hundred and ninety-ninth time that gets him every time. Because when you get up for the 200th time, he realizes it will be your last time and that you don't care how many times you go around, you're not giving up – ever. (We had a good laugh.)

Don't be discouraged. Keep getting up after every round. Be determined to last the whole fight. All fifteen rounds. The boxer, Rocky Balboa, kept taking the punches and surprised everyone by not staying down when he should have.

You may be feeling as if God thrown his hands up. Maybe loved ones or friends have, but God never will. He is here through every round and He is in your corner. You may be feeling that God has forsaken you because you feel so empty. You can't pray or sing or read your Bible much and you may be wanting to give up on the "God thing". But, that's when Jesus comes to you. When you are not faithful He is faithful. to His promises. He is longsuffering and patient and kind. He believes in you more than anyone in the world. Just don't give up on yourself. Day after day put your hope in God.

"It is of the Lord's mercies that we are not consumed because his compassions fail not. They are new every morning: great is thy faithfulness" (Lam. 3.23).

God's mercies are new every morning.

"…He who calls you is faithful" (I Thess. 5.24).

Moses thought he was disqualified after killing the Egyptian, but after 40 years, God still had a plan to use him as a deliverer. What has God called you to do? You are not disqualified if you have submitted your life to the Lord. He can still use you for His glory. He is faithful to His promises. He promises to never give up or leave. He has a plan and a future for you.

Prayer: Lord, thank You for Your faithfulness every morning. Thank You for Your mercies. I will trust in Your faithfulness and believe Your word.

———

Affirmation
God has great plans for me.
To give me a hope and a future,
to prosper me and not to hurt me.

———

Additional Scriptures:

"For I know the plans I have for you," says the Lord. "They are plans for good and not for disaster, to give you a future and a hope" (Jer. 29.11).

"The temptations in your life are no different from what others experience. And God is faithful. He will not allow the temptation to be more than you can stand. When you are tempted, he will show you a way out so that you can endure" (1 Cor. 10.13)

"Endure suffering along with, as a good soldier of Christ Jesus" (2 Tim. 2.3).

"The Lord isn't really being slow about his promise as some people think. No he is being patient for your sake..." (2 Pet. 3.9).

"God is greater than our confidence when we lack confidence" (1 John 4.20).

Rescued

"For he has rescued us from the kingdom of darkness and transferred us into the kingdom of his dear Son, who purchased our freedom and forgave our sins."

~COLOSSIANS. 1.13

FOR MANY YEARS, even as a Christian, I lived in darkness. Fear kept me there. I would keep reliving the fear I experienced through trauma as a child. Reliving it would take me to a dark place of psychosis over and over again. After a while, the psychotic episodes became somewhat of an escape for me. Even though the psychosis was terrifying, I still thought it was better than dealing with the pain.

Then, one day when I knew I was about to go to that dark place of fear and pain, my Heavenly Father showed me a picture of a scripture I had read earlier that morning during my quiet time, Colossians 1.13. He showed me a picture of Jesus lovingly picking up a little girl (me) and gently carrying her from a place of darkness and into a place of indescribable light. He literally gave me a word picture of Him rescuing me from the kingdom of darkness and bringing me into His Kingdom.

Whenever I had a psychotic episode or became delusional, my greatest fear was that the Lord would leave me there and I would never get out. After He gave me that picture of His love and of what He did when I accepted Him as Lord, my life has never been the same, because I believed the truth of what He had done for me rather the lie of abandonment.

Back during the Cold War, the Soviets had spies known as "sleepers." They would come to the States, live among Americans, and raise a family while waiting for their orders to be activated. Then, they would move into action on the mission they were always trained and intended to accomplish. That is one of the strategies of the enemy. He implants a lie into our life through tragedy, usually during childhood, then uses an event to trigger that lie. The trigger activates the intents the enemy has for implanting that lie. We start to respond and act upon what has always been there. We begin to act on the lie and walk in darkness.

So we are lying if we say we have fellowship with God but go on living in spiritual darkness; we are not practicing in the truth. But if we are living in the light, as God is in the light, then we have fellowship with each other, and the blood of Jesus, his Son, cleanses us from all sin (1 John 1.6, 7).

If we have fellowship with God, we cannot continue to walk in spiritual darkness. We have fellowship with God through His Son, Jesus. God is light and in Him there is no darkness at all. It is through fellowship with Him that we can walk in the light as He is in the light. Through fellowship with Him, and others, we can walk in the truth He reveals to us. I was walking in darkness because I had not experienced truth of His word. The devil didn't want me to know that I was rescued. He kept showing me the lie and I kept believing it. When I chose to believe the truth, I experienced the freedom that Jesus purchased for me.

I believe that many of the delusions I had during a manic or depressive episode was a result of a lie I believed as a child. When I became stressed or when someone did something to me, it triggered that trauma and set into motion a pattern of thoughts. I kept reliving the same delusion because of the pain that was never dealt with. Jesus knew the root of the issue and spoke to it through this one verse. Many of God's people are traumatized as children and live in that place of darkness even after salvation. They never realize that God has rescued them. He has truly rescued us from the kingdom of darkness and transferred, even carried us into the Kingdom of light.

Get a picture of this truth down inside your heart. You are rescued. You are delivered regardless of what you are experiencing now. Ask the Lord where the root of some type of lie or fear is and He will reveal it to you. The Lord will not leave you in that place of darkness. When you call out to Him, He will come and reveal Himself to you.

Prayer: Lord, thank You for rescuing me from the power of darkness and bringing me into Your kingdom of light. Show me how to walk in the light as You are in the light and resist the darkness.

———•———

Affirmation
I am a chosen generation, a royal priesthood, a holy nation and I will show forth the praises of Him who has called me out of darkness into His marvelous light.

———•———

Scriptures to meditate on:

"*But you are not like that, for you are a chosen people. You are royal priests, a holy nation, God's very own possession. As a result, you can show others the goodness of God, for he called you out of the darkness into his wonderful light*" (1 Pet, 2.9).

"*To open their eyes, so they may turn from darkness to light and from the power of Satan to God. They will receive forgiveness for their sins and be given a place among God's people, who are set apart by faith in me*" (Acts 26.18).

"*For once you were full of darkness, but now you have light from the Lord. So live as people of light! For this light within you produces only what is good and right and true*" (Eph. 5.8).

Redeemed from the Curse

"Christ purchased our freedom [redeeming us] from the curse (doom) of
the law [and its condemnation] by [Himself] becoming a curse for us,
for it is written [in the scriptures], Cursed is everyone who hangs from
a tree (is crucified)"

~GALATIANS 3.13, AMP

RELIGION USED TO drive my life and actions. Everything I did was out of duty and obligation. I lived my life according to the law and religion rather than through love, grace and faith. Religion gave me a sense of control. My life of works meant that I believed that my salvation. Everything was up to me not God.

Because I lived a life of works rather than relationship there was an ever-present sense of doom and condemnation.

"For when I tried to keep the law, it condemned me" (Gal. 2.19).

Living a life of works only fed my feelings of condemnation because it was all based on my efforts to please God and satisfy His requirements. In and of ourselves we could never satisfy the requirements of the law. Only Christ could do that and He did by dying on the cross. The law only makes us conscious of sin it never pays the penalty for it.

I was sexually abused as a child and felt that the only way God would be pleased is through my works or through my performance. Many people who have been sexually abused live a life based on performance. It is difficult for them to grasp the concept of the finished work of the cross. Religion and works appealed to me because it gave me a sense that I could finally gain approval and acceptance through my own actions and performance. Relinquishing that control meant trusting God for what He did, not what I did.

"God saved you by his grace when you believed. And you can't take credit for this; it is a gift from God" (Eph. 2.8, 9).

In my world, if I accepted a gift, there were always strings attached, something expected in return. It was strange for me to just receive God's gift, which is all He requires of us.

"But those who depend on the law to make them right with God are under his curse, for the Scriptures say, 'Cursed is everyone who does not observe and obey all the commands that are written in God's Book of the Law.' So it is clear that no one can be made right with God by trying to keep the law. For the Scriptures say, 'It is through faith that a righteous person has life'" (Gal. 3.10-12).

I constantly struggled with feelings of anxiety and I couldn't understand why. What I feared and dreaded the most was that I would, somehow, not please God. I also felt hopeless and helpless. To try to get rid of those feelings I lived my life full of religious actions, neglecting a real relationship with Christ. The more I tried to fulfill every letter of the law and follow the rules, the more I fell short. The more I fell short, the more condemned I felt. When I did something wrong, rather than ask forgiveness and believe I was forgiven, I would begin working to gain that acceptance. It was a vicious, exhausting cycle and a dangerous way of thinking and living. Learning to trust Christ daily for my salvation was the beginning of a loving relationship with Him and at first it felt very scary.

Jesus doesn't want us to live our lives according to some rulebook that can be used as a ladder to get closer to God as if the more good works we do the closer we get. Salvation is not based on good deeds we can do to earn our way into God's good graces. It is only through Jesus Christ that we gain access to God's throne.

Being redeemed from the curse of the law means that I live according to the law of liberty and the law of Christ which is the law of love rather than the law of sin and death.

"For the whole law can be summed up in this one command: 'Love your neighbor as yourself.'" (Gal. 5.14).

Everything we do should be out of love and obedience to the Lord. Our motive for doing things is to obey God. Jesus said that if we love Him we would obey His commandments and His one commandment is for us to love. When we do things out of our love for God and obedience to Him rather than an effort to gain salvation then we live a life of liberty and freedom.

When we realize that Christ took the curse, the doom and condemnation and nailed it to the cross so that we could be free from it, then we can live free from fear and dread. Jesus went to the cross out of love for us. He paid the penalty for sin. We can trust that He has done everything for us. We are redeemed from the curse. No more curse of the law and trying to fulfill it ourselves!

Prayer: Heavenly Father, I thank You for redeeming me from the curse and doom and condemnation of the law. Thank You for fulfilling it's requirement and setting me free from the curse of the law.

———————

Affirmation
I am redeemed from the curse of the law.
I am set free from the curse. I live according to the law of liberty and the law of love.

———————

Scriptures to meditate on:

"*So now there is no condemnation to those who belong to Christ Jesus.*" *(Rom. 8.1)*

"*And we will receive from him whatever we ask because we obey him and do the things that please him. And this is his commandment. We must believe in the name of his Son, Jesus Christ, and love one another, just as he commanded us*" *(1 John 3.22).*

"*And as we live in God, our love grows more perfect. So we will not be afraid on the Day of Judgment, but we can face him with confidence because we live like Jesus here in this world*" *(1 John 4.17).*

One Little Word

"Just say a simple "Yes, I will" or "No, I won't". Anything beyond this
is from the evil one."

~Matthew 5.37

ONE TRIGGER FOR my depression is when there is a conflict between priorities, which may have been a result of trying not to disappoint or annoy someone instead of setting my boundaries. I find that many times my life is comprised of juggling priorities. More than one person needs me to do more than one thing at the same time. When this happens, I have to use a word I dislike using – the word "No".

One way to alleviate stress in my life is to simplify it. In order to do this effectively it is important for me to determine what my priorities are. Once they are established then I need to organize my life around my priorities. Discovering my purpose played a major part in helping me determine what my priorities in life were. Learning how to say "No" to the tyranny of the urgent enabled me to live my life according to what had an eternal impact.

I never liked to tell people "No" because I was such a people pleaser. I also have the spiritual gift of mercy, so it is a real weakness of mine to try to "keep the peace". My goal in life was to make everyone happy. That is a stressful way to live and eventually no one is happy. I would always agonize over how to tell someone "No" because it was usually something they did not want to hear. So I would say "No", but I would add an explanation with it. I would try to justify why and make sure that the person understood why I was saying "No". Jesus tells us to keep it simple "Yes" or "No". If we say "Yes" then we should be people of our word. If we commit to something, it is best to be faithful to it and do it with our whole heart or to just say "No" from the beginning.

Saying "No" is a great way to set boundaries in your life. My home is very important to Tony and me. We shed many tears, bled and sweat out many years in our home and God has blessed us and multiplied our joy because of it. So, when it comes to our home, I have to set boundaries when others come to stay. That is very difficult for me, because I want to make everyone comfortable and happy, however, it should not be at the expense of our family's comfort. I tend to want to "rescue" people and end up enabling some, mainly because, rather than tell them "No" and set those boundaries, I hand over everything and expect nothing in return, neglecting other relationships in the process. (I said I wasn't going to get into the whole co-dependency thing, but sorry, I had to bring it up.)

Now, when we say "No" to someone we should never be rude or mean. We can learn how to be tactful, sweet and pleasant when we have to decline an invitation to participate in something. We should always respect authority and honor those in leadership.

The most difficult people to say "No" to for most of us are our family members. We need to learn how to say it and not feel guilty. Feeling guilty usually goes back to our need for approval from man. Once we know our God-given purpose, then we are not driven by our need for approval. We become people who want to redeem the time and make the most of every decision and make sure it has an eternal impact on our lives and the lives of those God has entrusted us with.

So practice saying "No" without feeling guilty. Try it with telemarketers. Ask the Lord before accepting any additional tasks. If He gives His OK, then do it with all of your heart. If there is some reservation (sometimes we may not understand why), then decline being confident that God approves of your decision even if others may not.

Prayer: Father, show me what is mine to do. My desire is to have an eternal impact in this world and to glorify You. Reveal Your Kingdom purpose to me that I may serve You with my whole heart.

Affirmation
I serve the Lord with gladness and with my whole heart. I live to please God and not man.

Scriptures to meditate on:

"Work willingly at whatever you do, as though you were working for the Lord rather than for people" (Col. 3.23)

"For we are God's masterpiece. He has created us anew in Christ Jesus, so we can do the good things he planned for us long ago" (Eph. 2.10).

"Servants, be obedient to them that are your masters according to the flesh, with fear and trembling in singleness of heart, as unto Christ. Not with eye service, as men pleasers; but as the servants of Christ, doing the will of God from the heart" (Eph. 6.5, 6).

Rejoice in the Lord

*"Yet I will rejoice in the Lord. I will exult in the [victorious] God of
my salvation! The Lord is my Strength, my personal bravery and my
invincible army; He makes my feet as hinds' feet and will make me to
walk [not stand in terror, but to walk] and make [spiritual] progress
upon my high places [of trouble, suffering, or responsibility]!"*

~HABAKKUK. 3.18,19, AMP

IT IS EASY to rejoice when everything is going well, but one important discipline
to learn is how to rejoice when everything is going wrong. I'm sure you have
already heard from well-meaning people who say all you need to do is rejoice
and your depression will leave. If there is something deeper, it will probably be
a process over time, not an overnight change. Rejoicing is something you do to
keep you from becoming paralyzed in fear and inactivity. It will help move you
forward toward healing.

*"Though the fig tree does not bud and there are no grapes on the vines, though
the olive crop fails and the fields produce no food, though there are no sheep in
the pen and no cattle in the stalls" (Hab. 3.17).*

In the above scripture text in Habakkuk, everything was going wrong. It was a
situation of desperation and lack. It actually looked like complete defeat. Have
you ever been in a place where it seemed like everything was going wrong?
When it looked like things couldn't get any worse? The first thing you want to

do is give up and feel sorry for yourself. It is times like these we need to learn how to rejoice in the Lord. We need to rejoice in the victorious God of our salvation.

How do we do that? By changing our focus from everything that is going wrong to our victorious God. If there is nothing else in your life to rejoice about, you can rejoice in the fact that you are saved and belong to Him. You can rejoice in the fact that Christ's victory is your victory.

"Thanks be to God who always leads us into triumph in Christ" (2 Cor. 2.14).

Regardless of how bad our situation may be, God always causes us to triumph over sin and the enemy. He is our victory and He is our strength. He is our invincible army. He is our personal bravery and will help us to make spiritual progress and to walk on our high places of trouble, suffering, or responsibility. Even when it feels like you are not making any spiritual progress, when you rejoice in the Lord, you can be confident that you are moving forward every time. When you get your focus on the Lord and all that He is doing, has done, and will do, then you can truly rejoice in Him. Even if you are struggling with depression, rejoice: "… we rejoice in the hope of the glory of God."(Rom. 5.2). Rejoice in the fact that you will not always feel this way. This, too, will pass.

What does rejoicing look like? It sounds like a song you sing under your breath at work or a song you hum in the shower or in the car. It is putting a smile on your face even when you feel like crying. It's finding something to compliment about someone, even when you feel horrible yourself. Most importantly, it's that smile that shows up on your face when you think of God's goodness or He shows you His love in a special way.

You may not even feel any joy. This is where your faith comes in. Begin to see yourself as joyful. Joy is a fruit of the Spirit (Gal. 2.20). It is a characteristic that needs to be developed over time and it is in you. It just may be small because it is a little "tapped out". It is still there, though. Develop that ripe fruit that you and others may enjoy and where God will be glorified.

This kind of joy isn't necessarily the jumping up and down until I feel happy or my circumstances change kind of dance. It is a warm, confident assurance of knowing you are loved and cared for. Like a blanket being wrapped affectionately around a lover, like the thawing of the winter with the anticipation of Spring. It is an inner knowing that will persevere through the night until dawn. It is a trusting and anticipation of knowing that dawn will come that brings a smile to your face.

There were many times when I needed "hind's feet" spoken about in Habakkuk 3.19 to make it through the day.

The hind is a female red deer whose home is in the mountains. The rear feed hind steps in exactly the same place as the front feet when climbing a mountain. She is the most sure-footed mountain animals. Her footing is focused and consistent.

"He makes me as surefooted as a deer enabling me to stand on mountain heights"
(Ps. 18.33).

I need hind's feet to make it through my times of suffering and to help me perform my responsibilities. For me, medication helps me to keep my footing sure on the mountains of life.

Some of you may need to see a doctor and talk to him about your symptoms. We can't will ourselves to think right when the brain that houses the mind is not working well, especially when it comes to brain injury. So, if the thoughts persist, please see a doctor. Depression or thoughts of suicide is sometimes the warning light that something is wrong with our bodies. Suicidal thoughts are the exception, not the rule, when it comes to our thinking.

After going to the doctor, some of you may need to temporarily take medication. Trust your doctor's wisdom. The medications should only be for a season. Sometimes, we are just going through a particular season of depression. We don't understand why. But, the lack of joy is definitely a warning light that something is wrong. We are a joyful people, so not being joyful is definitely out of the ordinary. Now that I know what joyfulness is, when I sense the heaviness, I don't assume anything. The first question I do ask, though, is "Am I doing too much?" Usually, if I "slow my roll", I find my joy and strength is renewed.

We have victory over the devil and he has to flee when we use our spiritual weapons. One of our weapons is wisdom.

"Wisdom calls aloud in the street, she raises her voice in the public squares; at the head of the noisy streets she cries out, in the gateways for the city she makes her speech" (Prov. 1.20, 21).

"Wisdom is all around us. It speaks through our loved ones, doctors, Pastors and even unbelievers, when we refuse to listen. God will generously give us wisdom when we ask." (Jas. 1.5)

Make an effort to rejoice in the Lord. This is not easy because you won't feel like it and you may feel heavy. Remember this is a process, though, not an overnight fix. Don't get discouraged. Things will change over time, and as you rejoice, you will find that God has given you "hinds' feet" to walk, not stand in terror, but to walk on your high places.

"My child, I am the God of your salvation. I will be your Strength today. I will help you to walk on your high places of responsibilities for I am your ever present help. I am your victory and your banner. I will go before you today and lead and guide you into triumph as I have promised. Hang in there. This, too, shall pass."

———◆———

Affirmation
God is my Strength, my Rock, and my invincible army. No weapon formed against me shall prosper. He always leads me into triumph in Christ. I am victorious in Him.

———◆———

Scriptures to meditate on:

"Always be full of joy in the Lord. I say it again — rejoice!" (Phil. 4.4)

"Because you are my helper, I sing for joy in the shadow of your wings" (Ps. 63.7).

"In him our hearts rejoice, for we trust in his holy name" (Ps. 33.21).

"Weeping may last for a night, but joy comes with the morning" (Ps. 30.5).

Give Thanks

"Thank [God] in everything [no matter what the circumstances may be, be thankful and give thanks], for this is the will of God for you [who are] in Christ Jesus [the Revealer and Mediator of that will]."

~1 THESSALONIANS 5.18, AMP

THERE WAS A time when I felt so depressed that I couldn't feel the Lord's presence at all. I actually felt like I was experiencing the wrath of God and I didn't even belong to Him anymore. It was such a scary feeling. I checked my life and would confess every sin I knew, but the symptoms remained. When someone would pray for me I would feel better, but when I was alone, those fearful feelings would return. What was I going to do? No one was around to pray for me and I couldn't keep calling someone. It was at this point that I learned how to be thankful for the most important thing—my salvation. It's not based on how I feel, but on what Christ did at Calvary.

Sometimes when we are suffering we think that God simply suggests that we should give thanks. He doesn't suggest it, He commands us to do so. Not to add to our suffering, but for our benefit. Giving thanks helps us keep our lives in perspective and keep our focus on things that will lift us out of a pit of depression rather than keep us in despair.

God tells us in His word to give thanks in every circumstance. Giving thanks in the midst of difficulties or adversity activates our faith in God. It keeps our faith in the One who is greater than our feelings of fear and condemnation. Giving thanks is an act that pleases God and gives Him an invitation to work on our behalf. Regardless of how difficult our situation, there is always something we can be thankful for (Hab. 3.17, 18).

Once I had a depressive episode that lasted about nine months. I couldn't seem to come out of it. I remember at one point, during my prayer times, all I could pray was, "Thank You for Your goodness. Thank You for Your mercy." I told a friend this was all I could pray and she said "Well, the word tells us to enter His gates with thanksgiving and that is what you are doing." It was so encouraging to see myself actually entering into God's presence through thanksgiving. After thanking God, I would spend the rest of the time in silence. I didn't realize it then, but those times of silence became a secret place for me and Jesus to meet each day and just sit.

I had to learn how to thank God just for being who He was instead of making it some sort of rain dance to get Him to make me feel better. I had to get to the point where I was going to serve God whether things got better or not.

Thanksgiving and a thankful heart is an attitude. It is a positive attitude. It is a way of thinking that is the opposite of complaining. Thanksgiving opens the door for God to work for us. It is so easy for us to see what's wrong rather than what's right and what we say out of our mouth will either work for us or against us. We need to make sure that our mouth is filled with thanksgiving to the Lord.

"I will bless the Lord at all times, His praise shall continually be in my mouth"
(Ps. 34.1).

Even when our emotions are down or out of sorts, we need to exercise the discipline or muscle of thanksgiving and having a thankful heart. It will bless God, ourselves, and everyone around us.

In Thessalonians it says to "pray without ceasing" (1 Thessalonians 5.17). Having a prayerful attitude filled with thanksgiving will help us get through many dark days. There may be times when you are thanking God through tears, but He still gets the glory through your words and through the tears. He actually puts them in a bottle.

"You keep track of all my sorrows. You have collected all my tears in your bottle. You have recorded each one in your book" (Ps. 56.8).

Give thanks to the Lord for He is good and His mercy and loving-kindness endures forever (1 Chronicles 16.34). If there is anything we can be thankful for, it's that His mercy and love endures. We may not feel lovable, but God still loves us. His love will never fail and His mercies are new every morning. Psalms 23. 6 says, "Surely, goodness and mercy shall follow me all the days of my life." Imagine that. I couldn't run from His goodness and mercy, even if I tried.

Thanksgiving brings joy. One way to focus on thankfulness to God is to write down all of the things in our lives we are thankful for. I know it seems like just a simple exercise, but it helps us to remind ourselves of just how good God is to us. So offer up the sacrifice of praise today. It is good to give thanks.

Prayer: I give thanks to You today, Father. Thank You for who You are. I am reminded of Your promises and Your love for me and I thank You most for that. I will bless You at all times. I give praise to You. Let the words of my mouth and the meditations of my heart be a pleasing sacrifice to You.

God's word to you: My goodness and mercy follow you. I will forever chase you down and never give up on you. You are mine and worth all of my love and attention. My eyes are only for you. Let's spend time sitting together in silence. Be still and know that I am God.

———◆———

Affirmation:
I will bless the Lord at all times. I give thanks to the Lord for His love endures forever. His praise will continually be in my mouth.

———◆———

Scriptures to meditate on:

"And give thanks to everything to God the Father in the name of our Lord Jesus Christ" (Eph. 5.20).

"Let all that I am praise the Lord; with my whole heart, I will praise his holy name. Let all that I am praise the Lord; may I never forget the good things he does for me. He forgives all my sins and heals all my diseases" (Ps. 103.1-3).

"Let us come to him with thanksgiving. Let us sing psalms of praise to him" (Ps. 95.2).

"Enter his gates with thanksgiving; go into his courts with praise. Give thanks to him and praise his name" (Ps. 100.4).

A Living Sacrifice

"So here's what I want you to do, God helping you: Take your every-day, ordinary life — your sleeping, eating, going-to-work, and walk-ing-around life—and place it before God as an offering. Embracing what God does for you is the best thing you can do for him."

~ROMANS *12.1, MSG*

ONE WAY TO be a living sacrifice is living a thankful life. Being a living sacrifice and thankfulness go hand in hand. One picture of both that is given in the Old Testament is the practice of giving a thank offering. It is the same thank offering that God asked of Abraham when He told him to sacrifice Isaac, His only son, and it is the same sacrifice that Jephthah vowed in the book of Judges (Judg. 11. 29-40).

In Leviticus whenever someone was thankful for a bountiful crop or for any favor God had shown, a voluntary thank offering could be offered in thanks to God. A lamb was sacrificed on the altar and was offered as a burnt offering.

"Jephthah made a vow before God: "If you give me a clear victory over the Ammonites, then I'll give to God whatever comes out of the door of my house to meet me when I return in one piece from among the Ammonites—I'll offer it up in a sacrificial burnt offering." Then Jephthah was off to fight the Ammonites. And God gave them to him. He beat them soundly, all the way from Aroer to the area around Minnith as far as Abel Keramim—twenty cities! A massacre! Ammonites brought to their knees by the People of Israel. Jephthah came home

to Mizpah. His daughter ran from the house to welcome him home—dancing to tambourines! She was his only child. He had no son or daughter except her. When he realized who it was, he ripped his clothes, saying, "Ah, dearest daughter—I'm dirt. I'm despicable. My heart is torn to shreds. I made a vow to God and I can't take it back!" She said, "Dear father, if you made a vow to God, do to me what you vowed; God did his part and saved you from your Ammonite enemies." And then she said to her father, "But let this one thing be done for me. Give me two months to wander through the hills and lament my virginity since I will never marry, I and my dear friends" (Judg. 11.29-37).

In Judges we see Jephthah make a vow to offer a burnt offering to God to thank Him for the victory over the Ammonites, however the burnt offering turned out to be his one and only daughter. He made a vow to give a voluntary thank offering and could not go back on it. It meant offering up his only child as a living sacrifice. She willingly obeyed after grieving the death of her dream of having children.

The message version of Romans 12.1 has captured the idea and lifestyle of someone who is a living sacrifice to the Lord. We are to present our ordinary, everyday lives as an offering to God. Everyday we should seek God and allow Him to use us throughout the day. Each day our lives should be thank offerings to God, holy and acceptable.

There was a time in my life when I thought spending the day in prayer in my room was what being a living sacrifice was all about. I thought it was acceptable to pray rather than clean my house, do laundry, or have dinner ready for my family. Prayer actually became an escape from all of the mundane things I needed to do. "Happy Homemaker" I was not, so rather than present these ordinary duties to the Lord on a daily basis, thankfully and praying as I did all of my duties throughout the day, I religiously set aside time to spend with Him, excluding everything else I needed to do.

I was so depressed, thinking about how uneventful my life seemed to be. How I would be so much happier working or getting out of the house. Although it may have been a blessing to my children, I see now that staying home full time was not the best thing I could have done and was going against how God made me, which contributed greatly to my depression. Tony and I realize now that staying home out of guilt and not recognizing that working outside the home was just as God-honoring as working within was very counterproductive to my efforts to be a great mom. To overcome the depression, I had to allow God to validate me and realize everything I offered to Him throughout the day was acceptable to Him.

I also had to recognize that I needed to grieve over the loss of some of my dreams of having a career in the corporate world, just like Jephthah's daughter grieved over not being able to have children because of the sacrifice of her life for her father. She took two months to mourn over her loss.

There may be a brief period of depression when you are grieving over the loss of a dream, even though you are in God's will and obeying him. God is not a heartless God. He knows what He is asking us to do. He's asking us to trust Him and knows that being a living sacrifice is not easy, but we can offer ourselves up to God in love, adoration and thanksgiving as Christ did for us.

When Tony and I decided to adopt two toddlers, I had to say goodbye to the empty nest I was so close to and the dream of traveling around the world once the kids were gone. I felt guilty because, even though I knew we were in the will of God, it was a painful process of dying to my own will. I had to get to the point where I was thankful and ready to lay it all down. This took a while, and I don't think we should feel guilty when it does, because once the process is done, there is no place we would rather be than in the will of God. When we are honest and count the cost, we are willing to pay the price when the time comes.

After the adoption of our sons, I was home full-time again. I was once again in that season when there were days when all I could do was get out of bed and get the bare minimum done to, take care of the boys. I learned to offer the little I did do as a living sacrifice. I couldn't get overwhelmed with my "To Do List". I had to offer all the everyday things to the Lord and know that His grace will cover all the things I didn't get done.

Present all of your accomplishments for the day as a bouquet of flowers every evening and all your hopes, plans and dreams as an offering to God. A sweet smelling savor as you pray throughout the day. Thanking Him for all He does, through our obedience, brings great joy to the Father.

———————

Affirmation
You are completely accepted, pleasing and approved by God. You are His
glorious treasure and trophy.

———————

Prayer: Lord, I present my life to You as a living sacrifice today. I place my life into Your hands. I live my life in a way that is pleasing to You. Help me to fulfill Your will and purpose today.

Scriptures to meditate on:

"For God bought you with a high price. So you must honor God with your body" (*I Cor. 6.20*).

"God paid a high price for you, so don't be enslaved by the world" (*I Cor. 7.23*).

Be Transformed

"Don't copy the behavior and customs of this world, but let God trans-form you into a new person by changing the way you think. Then you will learn to know God's will for you, which is good and pleasing and perfect."

~ROMANS *12.2*

EVERYONE IS INTO remodeling these days. There is always a kitchen or bathroom or bedroom that needs an overhaul. I love watching the Home and Garden network. I get some great ideas for remodeling and decorating. There's just one problem. I never start any of those projects for my home. I get great ideas, but never apply them. If I did, my home would look like a palace.

The same is true with our thinking. When we spend time remodeling our thought life, our lives become things of beauty from the inside out. It is not enough to read great books or even the Bible. We have to apply what we hear and read to our own lives. (Jas 1. 22-25).

On television it looks like projects are done in just the time it takes to watch the program, but in reality, many projects take months to finish. With our thought life it is a never-ending process of changing the way we think. Once we finish one room it is time to move on to another. Each phase takes time and dedication.

I know that the reason why I have not done any decorating or remod-eling projects in my own home is because I get overwhelmed with the size of the projects. I never start, rather than start and never complete it.

Sometimes we feel like we are such a mess that we never begin the process of transformation. We feel hopeless when we think of all the work we need to do.

For years I was in the habit of negative thoughts, especially when I was in a depressive mood. Even when I was in a normal mood and everything was in balance, I had to change some of my habitual ways of thinking. For instance, I had to change the way I thought about myself. I always considered myself as weak because I struggled with mental illness. God didn't see me as weak. I had to change my way of thinking to what God said about me, not what I felt and thought about myself for years. It was a never ending cycle that needed to be broken. It wasn't until I began making changes in the way I thought that the transformation began. I first had to recognize the bad habits that were not consistent with the Bible, then I began to make daily changes that would last a lifetime and would bring me closer to complete wholeness. If you start with little daily steps towards applying simple principles, then you will find that over time you are closer to the whole person you want to be.

One way I always get ideas for remodeling is by looking in magazines to get a picture of what I want the finished project to look like. Do you have a picture in mind of what your wholeness will look like? As a man thinks in his heart so is he (Prov. 23.7). Is it based on what the Bible says we should resemble or on the world's idea of success? Get a picture in your mind of what you want to look like in a year. Think of yourself as a house. What areas need repair? What areas need attention? Are there past hurts or wounds that need healing? Then begin dealing with them through a godly relationship or through counseling. Don't be afraid to get help. Much of the work cannot be done alone.

How do you want to act? Write down areas that you need the Lord to help you with and find out what the Bible says about them. Begin the process of remodeling today and realize that it is a time-consuming process. Don't let setbacks, mistakes or delays discourage you. Start the process and allow God's Word to transform your life into something beautiful.

Prayer: Heavenly Father, show me the areas in my life that need work. Transform my life from the inside out. I make a choice today to be conformed into the image of Your dear Son. I am not my own, I am bought with a price. I am totally Yours.

———————

Affirmation:
You are predestined to be conformed into the image of Christ. Your life is being beautified as you change your way of thinking.

———————

Scriptures to meditate on:

"For God knew his people in advance, and he chose them to become like his Son, so that his Son would be the firstborn among many brothers and sisters" (Rom. 8.29).

"So all of us who have had that veil removed can see and reflect the glory of the Lord. And the Lord — who is the Spirit — makes us more and more like him as we are changed into his glorious image" (2 Cor. 3.18).

"Anyone who listens to my teaching and follows it is wise, like a person who builds a house on solid rock. Though the rain comes in torrents and the floodwaters rise and the winds beat against that house, it won't collapse because it is built on bedrock" (Matt. 7.24, 25).

"We use God's mighty weapons, not worldly weapons, to knock down the strongholds of human reasoning and to destroy false arguments" (2 Cor. 10.5).

No Worries

Don't worry about anything; instead, pray about everything. Tell God what you need, and thank him for all he has done. Then you will experience God's peace, which exceeds anything we can understand. His peace will guard your hearts and minds as you live in Christ Jesus.

~PHILIPPIANS *4.6, 7*

ANXIETY IS A symptom of depression. For years I thought anxiety was inescapable. I never associated it with depression. For me, medication gave me relief from something I thought was just me, but even after it was prescribed I still needed to overcome the habit of worrying.

Crowds are very stressful for me. I usually try to stay away from them, however sometimes this cannot be avoided. My husband loves crowds. He can really "work a room". I, on the other hand, have to take a deep breath and take things one person at a time and try not to allow the space to close in on me. I have to smile and really try to concentrate on being friendly and on making conversation.

Anxiety is caused by worry: worry about the past or dread of the future. Staying in the present is difficult to do when you are constantly preoccupied with what happened in the past and worried about it happening again, or with the future, worrying about the unknown. Awareness of the "now" or the present is the best way to deal with anxious thoughts. Realizing that all the "what if" scenarios is often a ploy of the enemy to get us anxious about the unknown. It is a "peace stealer."

I can be a major worrier. I worry about my children, my finances, my health, just about anything and everything. The only thing that combats it is prayer. Not just worried prayers, but finding my answer in the Bible and praying the promises of God. Actually casting my cares on the Lord before the anxious thoughts take charge is the best strategy. One thing to do is pray through all of the "What if's". I had to get into the habit of praying about everything that is on my heart. I had to learn how to receive the peace of God. I had to actually see myself giving my bundle of worries to the Lord and unloading it onto Him for good. Journaling and writing lists tends to help me. I had to develop a confidence that God was in control of every situation I found myself in and that all things worked together for my good (Romans 8.28).

Prayer helps us stay in the "now." I cannot change the past but I can affect the future by praying right now. I can activate my faith right now by praying to God and thanking Him for all He has done. Remembering how He has helped me in the past encourages me to believe Him for what I need right now.

There are times when I pray through the day. By praying about everything and expecting God's peace to come, I am able to get through the present anxiety. Sometimes it is an anxiety or panic attack and my prayers are no more than, "Jesus, please help me." I can remember days of nothing but anxiety and worry. There was no peace and I just suffered in silence thinking God didn't hear my feeble prayers. God hears us. He is attentive to our prayers, even the ones we whisper in the supermarkets with 50 people standing around us. We can cast every care on Him knowing He cares for us (1 Pet. 5.7). Praying through your worries and cares is how we resist the devil and cause him to flee (Jas 4.7). The feelings may not go away instantly, but our peace is the quiet assurance that God is with us, He hears and He cares. That peace keeps us from giving up and teaches us how to wait for the feelings of calm to follow. Even when it seems like there is no relief, continue to stand and resist and press against the worry. Hanging on through every wave of anxiety develops perseverance.

Stress is usually the trigger to most anxiety. It is those times when you do need to get away and take the time to relieve the stress that your body is under. Research shows that it takes less than 30 seconds to relieve stress. Here are a few tips:

- Take the time to put on some lotion that smells good or that is relaxing.
- Take the time to sit with relaxing music and focus on all the good things that God is doing.
- A simple thing like taking a bath can make a huge difference. If you don't have time to take a bath, take a shower in the dark with candles lit.
- Quiet your mind and spirit and allow the Lord to minister peace.
- Try some relaxation or breathing to try to relieve the tension and stress that is in your body.
- Try to pinpoint what is causing the stress.
- Try to go to the same spot every day at the same time.

For years I would try to fight off the anxiety on my own without the help of medication for the depression. I don't believe that fight was mine to fight without some sort of help from medication. There are a few alternatives to medication. Here are a few:

- Go on a brisk walk, even a prayer walk. Say scripture or pray for your neighbors or family while you are walking.
- You have to get still. Do relaxation where it is quiet. Control your breathing and begin to meditate on scripture and play music with scripture, if possible.
- Prayer journal. Write all the things on your mind that are worrying you, stressing you out or bothers you. Afterwards, write your praise and thanksgiving to God.

For me, I needed medication because my disease was clinical and caused by a physical "misfires" in my brain. After resisting for years, when I received the medication to deal with the depression then the anxiety went away. But, even with the medication I needed to break the habit of worry that sometimes brought on the anxiety. Medication only brought me to the point where I could hear the Holy Spirit clearly and understand Him. There was still a transformation that needed to take place in my thinking. There were times when I would actually pace the floor with anxious thoughts. I had to stop and think about what was bothering me and take all my worries to the Lord one by one. Being still is the first thing you can do to combat anxiety.

Some people have what is called General Anxiety Disorder (GAD). Sometimes, even with the medication, they get no relief. Jesus knows how to get to the root of any issues that may be causing the anxiety and bring relief. It is through prayer and truly developing a relationship with Him that we can get to the root of our symptoms. He promises us peace when our thoughts are fixed on Him and He cannot lie.

It is difficult to trust someone you don't know. It is also difficult to trust God when everyone else in your life has let you down. But, God invites us to trust Him with all of our hearts and promises to never let us down.

It's true. He really does give us peace when we take our eyes off our circumstances and focus our attention on Him. There is a place of rest we can enter into. It is a place of trust we can stay in where we are totally trusting in the Lord, trusting in His sovereignty and His character. We can know that everything will work together for our good and that God is in complete control.

So shift your focus today. Find that place where you can sit and think on all of the good things God has done for you. Think on all the good things in life. He will bring you peace. I have five children so I know how difficult this can be, but you need to let your family know that you need just a few minutes alone.

"Give your burdens to the Lord and he will take care of you. He will not permit the godly to slip and fall" (Ps. 55.22)

Then, turning to his disciples, Jesus said, "That is why I tell you not to worry about everyday life — whether you have enough food to eat or enough clothes to wear. For life is more than food and your body more than clothing. Look at the ravens. They don't plant or harvest or store food in barns, for God feeds them. And you are far more valuable to him than any birds! Can all your worries add a single moment to your life? And if worry can't accomplish a little thing like that, what's the use of worrying over bigger things? And don't be concerned about what to eat and what to drink. Don't worry about such things. Those things dominate the thoughts of unbelievers all over the world, but your Father already knows your needs" (Luke 12.22-26, 29, 30)

"Be still in the presence of the Lord, and wait patiently for him to act" (Ps. 37.7a).

If you are really in a panic, call a friend or your therapist. It is alright to ask for help.

Prayer: *Thank You that you are with me and will never leave me nor forsake me. I submit myself to You and receive Your peace. I resist the devil and He will flee. Thank You for Your peace and for helping me.*

———•———

Affirmation
Cast all your cares on the Lord for He cares. Believe and know He hears and will give you the requests of my heart. Pray about everything.

———•———

Scriptures to meditate on:

"And we are confident that he hears us whenever we ask for anything that pleases him. And since we know he hears us when we make our requests, we also know that he will give us what we ask for" (I John 5.14, 15).

"But if you remain in me and my words remain in you, you may ask anything you want, and it will be granted!" (John 15.7).

"You can ask for anything in my name, and I will do it, so that the Son can bring glory to the Father" (John 14.13).

"From the ends of the earth, I cry to you for help when my heart is overwhelmed. Lead me to the towering rock of safety" (Ps. 61.2).

"When doubts filled my mind, your comfort gave me renewed hope and cheer" (Ps. 94.19).

Grace Walk

"God saved you by his grace when you believed. And you can't take credit for this; it is a gift from God. Salvation is not a reward for the good things we have done, so none of us can boast about it."

~EPHESIANS *2.8, 9*

God's grace is sufficient. (2 Cor. 12.9)

IT IS SO important to walk in the grace of God. His grace enables us to do what He wants us to do for His glory. For years I walked in legalism and religion. I questioned my salvation on a regular basis because I based my salvation on works rather than grace.

One of the symptoms of bipolar is guilt. I felt guilty all the time. I was obsessed with perfection and performance, and therefore, didn't have much grace for others.

One of the lies of the enemy is that you have fallen from grace. But, that is when you have to trust that God's grace is sufficient, that His grace and love is enough. You have to learn how to rest in what He has already provided and trust in His completed work.

When I received the revelation of this verse of scripture, that my salvation was not based on works, but the grace of God and that it was a gift, it changed my whole way of thinking. I didn't know how to receive gifts, so I had to learn how to receive God's grace. I had to stop working my way to

Heaven and just relax. I had to trust God totally for my salvation. I was so sad when I realized my actions were saying that I didn't trust God for my salvation. I was actually walking in unbelief and doubt by trying to win His approval through works.

Walking in grace meant that I believed that I already had God's approval because I believed in Christ. It meant that when I did something wrong that I said I was sorry, repented, believed I was forgiven and continued on with my day, regardless of how I felt. It also meant that I hadn't fallen from grace because I was going through depression. Regardless of how I felt, I had to trust what God said and that my sins were as far as the East is from the West.

At first, this felt awkward. I was so tempted to run up to my room and begin praying for forgiveness every 20 minutes. That was a temptation for me. Not the fact that I was praying. I cried out the Lord and prayed constantly against the temptation to drop everything and run to my room and hide. I had to resist because walking by works opened the door to the enemy. It only led to more condemnation and fear.

Are you living a life of works? Are you walking in God's grace and love today? What is your grace walk like? Are you boasting about all that you do for God and hoping that it will get you to Heaven? Are you comparing yourself to others and thinking you're better because, "At least I don't do such in such."? When our grace walk becomes religious, we become religious towards others and self-righteous. This is just as dangerous as feelings of guilt.

Walking in grace is not all about your works and religious acts, it is truly about receiving God's gift of salvation and adoption. Nothing more.

Prayer: Lord, Your grace is all I need today. Help me be aware of Your marvelous grace and let it be the foundation that my faith is built upon. Shower me with your blessings, now and forever more. Amen.

------•------

Affirmation
I am saved by grace through faith. it is a gift that I gladly receive. His grace is sufficient to sustain me. I glory in my infirmities that the power of God may rest upon me.

------•------

Scriptures to meditate on:

"I do not treat the grace of God as meaningless. For if keeping the law could make us right with God, then there was no need for Christ to die." (Gal. 2.21)

"For if you are trying to make yourselves right with God by keeping the law, you have been cut off from Christ! You have fallen away from God's grace." (Gal. 5.4)

"Each time he said, 'My grace is all you need. My power works best in weakness.' So now I am glad to boast about my weaknesses, so that the power of Christ can work through me." (2 Cor. 12.9)

Perfect Peace

"You will keep in perfect peace all who trust in you, all whose
thoughts are fixed on you! Trust in the LORD always for the LORD
GOD is the eternal Rock."

~Isaiah *26.3, 4*

ANXIETY CAN BE overcome through prayer and changing your focus. Not right away, but slowly over time.

That is not easy to do when your mind wanders and races and you cannot concentrate on anything. It is especially difficult to sleep when you have anxious thoughts. But, you can train yourself to focus on one thing. Try focusing on one scripture or even a portion of one verse. Like, "In peace I will lie down and sleep." (Ps. 4.8) Begin to thank the Lord for safety and peace and sleep. Try not to think about all that you have to do the next day. Take no thought for tomorrow (Matthew 6.34). Focus on the present. Focus on the bed you are lying on. Focus on what you are feeling, seeing, smelling, and hearing. Thank God for all of it and think about the fact that He is with you, and He will never leave you. Talk to Him about all your fears and all your apprehension. Cast all of your cares on Him for He cares for you (1 Pet. 5.7).

Keeping our thoughts on the Lord truly keeps us in perfect peace. That is His promise. It is not easy to focus sometimes when you are working or driving, but with practice, you can learn how to focus your thoughts on the Lord and all that He has done. When you are breathing and doing relaxation exercises it is important to focus on the Lord and not open your mind up to just anything.

Your mind can get away from you and take you places you don't want to go. Relaxation is good to help you focus on the present. It can help you focus on what is happening right now and keep you from thinking about the past or the future that you may be dreading.

Whenever I begin to dread the future, I focus on the present. I begin to focus on what is happening with me right now. If it is a difficult situation then I begin to pray or journal my prayers when I can't even speak. In Philippians Paul tells us to be anxious for nothing and to pray about everything. He also tells us to think on specific things. Whatever is true, honest, just, pure, lovely, and a positive report (Phil. 4.8). He promises us peace when our thoughts are fixed on Him and He cannot lie.

It is difficult to trust someone you don't know. It is also difficult to trust God when everyone else in your life has let you down. But, God invites us to trust Him with all of our hearts and promises to never let us down.

It's true. He really does give us peace when we take our eyes off our circumstances and focus our attention on Him. There is a place of rest we can enter into. It is a place of trust we can stay in where we are totally trusting in the Lord, trusting in His sovereignty and His character. We can know that everything will work together for our good and that God is in complete control.

So shift your focus today. Find that place where you can sit and think on all of the good things God has done for you. Think on all the good things in life. He will bring you peace.

Prayer: Lord, help me to keep my eyes and thoughts fixed on You. I thank You for Your peace. I give all my tomorrows to You and cast all of my cares on You. I know You care for me.

Affirmation
I will fix my thoughts on God. I will lie down and sleep in peace and safety for the Lord keeps me safe.

"*May the* LORD *bless you*
and protect you.
May the LORD *smile on you*
and be gracious to you.
May the LORD *show you his favor*
and give you his peace. (Num. 6.24-26)

Faith Walk (Not Feelings)

"For we live by believing, not by seeing [our senses]".

~2 Corinthians. 5.7 (brackets mine)

SOMETIMES IT IS difficult to walk by faith and not by feelings, especially when those emotions are strong and convincing. It is hard to keep believing we are healed when we have symptoms that tell you otherwise. The devil comes during those times to discourage us and try to steal our faith. It is easy to feel like you are completely forsaken and that there is no hope of recovery. There are days when I ask the Lord, "When? When will the time come when I won't have to deal with these symptoms and not have to take medication?"

Frankly, that is the wrong question to ask. God is healing me right now. In Mark 16.18 says "And they shall lay hands on the sick, and they shall recover." The word "recover" means to mend or to change. There were times when I would go to the healing line and ask for prayer and they would lay hands on me and I would be discouraged when it "felt" like nothing changed.

It's the same when we decide to follow Christ. We can say a prayer with sincerity and simplicity and not feel a thing. Then, when we do something we know is not pleasing to God, we may give up and doubt our salvation. When it comes to healing (spiritual and physical) things do change – over time.

The mending process had begun in me. There are some people who would be in the same healing line and go to the doctor the next day and be taken off the medication right away. That is great, but don't get discouraged when your healing or change is not visible immediately. Believe God's Word and keep believing regardless of what you see or feel. "All the days of my appointed time will I wait, till my change come." (Job 14.14)

I have found that my healing is a journey. It is a process. We walk by faith. Day by day we live by faith. There is instantaneous healing and then there is the healing process. Neither form of healing is any less miraculous. God chooses which type of healing He wants to perform. We, of course, would prefer instantaneous evidence of healing. God requires something of us that is just as much an act of faith as prayer. We learn obedience through the things we suffer (Heb. 5.8). Like Paul, I want to know Him in the power of His resurrection and in the fellowship of His suffering (Phil. 3. 10).

Whenever I was suffering through an episode, it would feel as if God had gone and He was nowhere to be found. I couldn't feel His presence. I felt as if there was no connection at all with Him. It is at those times that I have to simply trust that God is with me. I have to trust that He is faithful to His promises. It is difficult when all of your senses are telling you that you are a complete failure, that God is mad at you or that you are completely without hope, but no matter what you may feel or see or hear or touch or smell, God is with you and He is not angry with you. Believe what He says about you. Choose to believe what His word says about your situation. That you are an overcomer and that He loves you.

How do you keep believing even though you don't see any results? Go by God's promises. Believe that this light affliction will reap a more eternal weight in glory (2 Cor. 4.17). We know that this earth, this life is not our home. We are just visiting. We trust in God's promise of healing even if we never see it in this life. We trust God's ways and His heart even when we don't understand.

Continue to stay on the healing journey and the faith walk. Walking in faith means walking in obedience to what God shows you to do. Are you taking medication? Then take it by faith. Are you seeing a therapist? Do it by faith knowing and believing that God is the ultimate Healer and Great Physician and pray that God gives him or her insight. Are you suffering with symptoms? Know that God is with you and will help you. Ask God what your part is in the process. Don't give up or stop believing what God says about your situation. Take a step of faith beyond your feelings.

Prayer: *Father, I believe You are the Great I AM. With you all things are possible. I know you are with me and healing me today. I will trust in You and not be afraid. Thank You for Your promises to me. You are faithful and true. Help me to stay on the healing journey.*

———•———

Affirmation
I will walk by faith and not my feelings today. I will wait until my change comes. God is faithful.

———•———

Scriptures to meditate on:

"Then Jesus said to the disciples, "Have faith in God. I tell you the truth, you can say to this mountain, 'May you be lifted up and thrown into the sea,' and it will happen. But you must really believe it will happen and have no doubt in your heart. I tell you, you can pray for anything and if you believe that you've received it, it will be yours" (Mark 11.22-24).

"God will make this happen, for he who calls you is faithful" (1 Thess. 5.24).

"Faith is the confidence that what we hope for will actually happen; it gives us assurance about things we cannot see" (Heb. 11.1).

"All these people died still believing what God had promised them. They did not receive what was promised, but they saw it all from a distance and welcomed it. They agreed that they were foreigners and nomads here on the earth" (Heb. 11.13).

"You can ask for anything in my name and I will do it, so that the Son can bring glory to the Father. Yes, ask me for anything in my name, and I will do it!" (John 14.13, 14)

Reaching Forward

*"I don't mean to say that I have already achieved these things or that I
have already reached perfection, But I press on to possess that perfection for which Christ Jesus first possessed me. No dear brothers and
sisters, I have not achieved it, but I focus on this one thing forgetting
the past and looking forward to what lies ahead."*

~Philippians 3.12,13

The one thing that can keep us from moving forward is our past. Sometimes we
have regrets and think, "Man, I wish I hadn't done that." There are many things
in my past that I wish I hadn't done. Things I did when I was in a psychotic state,
a depressive episode or a manic episode (even in remission). There was a time
when I thought I would never live any of those things down and it kept me from
moving on with my life.

But the Word of God says that we should forget those things that are behind
and press toward the mark of the prize. Trust me, it is a process once you decide
to forget the past. The devil doesn't want you to forget and sometimes friends
and family members won't let you forget either.

Paul is the writer of the scripture above. Think about all that he did before his salvation. He was a murderer and persecuted the church and had a
violent past, yet, he encourages us to reach forward. Even with all that he ac-
complished he still said that he hadn't arrived. What an encouragement to us
today. He encourages us to keep pressing toward what's ahead and that there
is a reward.

The word perfection here does not mean sinless perfection. It means our intent is to not miss the mark. The word "sin" means "to miss the mark". In Paul's time people knew the context of being an archer and working to hit the bull's eye in the middle of the target. Our purpose in life is to always aim for the bull's eye. We always want to love better, serve better and live the way God wants us to. We will miss the mark, no doubt, because we're not perfect, but our intention is always to keep our eyes on the mark: the bull's eye, and to do it we will need to work hard at it.

If you are going through depression, it is hard to press on to perfection when all you really want to do is just stay still, paralyzed in fear and dread. I remember days when just thinking about the day before brought me to a screeching halt. Or, just thinking about all that I needed to get done would simply overwhelm me. Reaching forward means that you have to trust in the scripture that says,

"Weeping may endure for a night, but joy comes in the morning" (Ps. 30.5).

You have to trust that if you get up one more day, the joy will come. Get up again and again and again. Don't give up, press forward with all your might.

Sometimes it is a past trauma that holds you paralyzed in fear. I think past trauma held me in a loop of despair and fear for years. I finally had to ask Jesus to speak into the trauma and heal the wound of it. He did take the trauma, even though I still have the memory of the event. That is something only God can do and He will when you ask Him. That past trauma doesn't have to haunt your life. God can remove it and help you to move forward. Don't this alone. It would be like trying to do surgery on yourself with a butter knife. You will always need help for this or it will be a bloody mess. Pray God brings someone into your life, maybe professionally or through your church, to pray with you. Even doing this will still be a process. Choosing to press forward is not easy, but can be done through God's strength.

Regardless of how you are feeling today, press toward the mark. It may start by you getting out of bed and making it so you don't get back in. Then taking it one step at a time until your day is done. God is with you through each step. He will be there when you close your eyes and when you open them tomorrow.

Keep reaching forward and if you fall back, reach again. There is a prize at the end.

I can't say that I have arrived, but I can encourage you to keep reaching forward and let you know that there is joy in the morning and that there is a prize. God brought me through and He will bring you through.

Prayer: Lord Jesus, help me to press on toward the bull's eye for this day and for the high calling you have on my life. I know that you have a hope and a future for me and I trust that you will bring it to pass in my life. As I sow in tears I know that I will reap in the reward of joy. Thank you for your promises, In Your name, Amen.

━━━◆━━━

Affirmation:
I forget the past and reach forward to what lies ahead. I know that it is good.

━━━◆━━━

Scriptures to meditate on:

"*Those who plant in tears will harvest with shouts of joy.*" *(Ps. 126.5)*

"*So let's not get tired of doing what is good. At just the right time we will reap a harvest of blessing if we don't give up.*" *(Gal. 6.9)*

"*But Jesus told him, 'Anyone who puts a hand to the plow and then looks back is not fit for the Kingdom of God'.*" *(Luke 9.62)*

Balancing the Extremes

*"Be well balanced (temperate, sober of mind) be vigilant and cautious
at all times; for the enemy of yours, the devil, roams around like a
lion roaring [in fierce hunger], seeking someone to seize upon and
devour."*

~I Peter 5.8, AMP

THERE IS A movement called "extreme sports". Every sport is done to the extreme. There is extreme skateboarding, motor cross, skiing and probably others I'm unaware of. I don't believe God wants us to live in the extremes. I believe He designed us to live a balanced life. I'm not saying we shouldn't be involved in extreme sports. I'm just using the analogy to make a point.

Dealing with Bipolar symptoms meant dealing with two extremes. I struggle with extreme highs and extreme lows. I think I go beyond just extreme highs and lows because I go so low that I would become delusional and so high I would become psychotic. Needless to say that whenever I was in one of those two extremes, the devil would begin prowling around me and my family. It made me vulnerable to his tactics, temptations and ploys. So one effective weapon God taught me was the concept of being well balanced. I had to learn to live a well-balanced life. Balanced eating, sleeping, exercising – everything, which is hard to do with a family of seven where everything is extremely busy, extremely loud and extremely fast.

Peter exhorts us to be well balanced, to have a temperate and sober mind. One way I applied this to some of my extreme states of mind was by becoming aware of when I was out of balance in my thinking. The most difficult part about doing this was to determine what was normal. Realizing that a chemical imbalance was the cause of my extreme moods and thoughts helped, too. For years I thought that all my mood swings were normal. I refused to stay on medication and this left me open to the devil in so many ways. When I finally began working with my doctor to adjust them, in addition to maintaining a balanced life, I functioned so much better.

Another way I stayed balanced was by not having too much or too little to do. I had to be aware of when my life got too hectic and needed to slow down and when I had too much idle time on my hands. Both extremes were dangerous.

When I am in a normal mood, I am vigilant and cautiously protecting my balanced lifestyle. Whenever I begin moving toward extremes, I first ask the Lord what caused it and He directs me toward ways to rectify it. It is most commonly lack of sleep. There are times when there are emotional triggers and the Lord needs to heal me of the wounds that trigger manic or depressive episodes, but as the Lord heals me emotionally it becomes more of a physical problem that could usually be dealt with through exercise, a peanut butter and jelly sandwich or a good night's sleep. Sometimes it takes an adjustment in my medication, which is often the last thing on my list, but for now, probably the most important.

Living with clinical depression or a chemical imbalance means that you are constantly making an effort to balance your brain's chemistry. There are so many factors that affect your brain. It could be emotional stress or diet or lack of sleep or any number of other contributors. Being aware of what affects your brain chemistry is half the battle. Knowing what throws you off balance is crucial.

"Fill in the valleys, and level the mountains and hills. Straighten the curves, and smooth out the rough places." (Is. 40.4)

God promises to make every valley exalted and every hill made low and that He would make the crooked places straight. He has done that in my life in a way that only He could. He wants us to live well-balanced lives. He doesn't want us living in extremes. It requires living cautiously and soberly and being aware of our bodies. We need to be aware of physiological changes and times of transition. We need to know our bodies and most of all, know our God. We need to truly be sensitive to the Holy Spirit. He will lead us and guide us into a more balanced way of living. I don't always get this right. It's a struggle with my husband and family, but I am thankful that God faithfully keeps me, even when the enemy is prowling.

So close those doors. Find out what normal is for you and cooperate with the Holy Spirit as He shows you your part in your healing.

Prayer: Lord, show me how to live a well-balanced life. Show me how to live carefully, wisely and be alert. Make every crooked place of imbalance smooth. In Your name, Amen

———————

Affirmation
I am watchful. I use self-control
and Iam sensitive to the Holy Spirit.

———————

Scriptures to meditate on:

So be on your guard, not asleep like others. Stay alert and be clearheaded. Night is the time when people sleep and drinkers get drunk. But let us who live in the light be clearheaded, protected by the armor of faith and love, and wearing as our helmet the confidence of our salvation. (1 Thess. 5:6-8)

"... Christ's love controls us..." (2 Cor. 5.14)

Closing the Doors

"Neither give place to the devil."

~*Ephesians 4.27*

ONCE YOU HAVE tasted freedom you don't want to go back to bondage. Once I was free I didn't want to go back to the way things were in the past. God set me free by His grace and mercy and love, but it is a partnership with the Holy Spirit to stay free. After God delivered me from my fears I had to close all the doors to the enemy and not give him opportunity to gain a foothold in my life.

One of the doors that I had to close was negative thoughts. I had to get into the habit of "casting down imaginations" and every argument against God (2 Cor. 10.5). I had to watch what I exposed my eyes and ears to. I couldn't watch everything on television or listen to any radio station. I had to close those doors that might allow fear and doubt to enter in.

As I mentioned in an earlier chapter, I also had to change my lifestyle. I had to make sure I got the rest that I needed and that I ate right, took my medication and exercised. When any of these areas are out of balance I begin to see the warning light come on and that warning light is often depression, especially when I am tired. When we adopted our two sons, there were weeks when I was sleep deprived. I would be up all night, but when they went down for a nap, I went down for a nap. That was a must for me to survive and keep myself functioning and to keep me out of the pit of depression. I still began to sink for a few weeks. My doctor tried different medications, but nothing worked so this was one of those times when I had to just hang on and go through. With the help of my husband and a few good friends, I made it. Nothing helped, though, like getting a few nights of good sleep.

God gives us wisdom to live our lives. He leads, guides and shows us any areas that we may be leaving an opportunity for Satan to work in our lives. Even though Christ has set us free through His mighty hand, we need to make sure that we stay free by cooperating with the Holy Spirit. I had to learn to be sensitive to the Holy Spirit and to my body and even be aware of my moods. When my mood was wrong I needed to take the time to ask the Lord what was causing the shift in my mood. I also had to listen to my husband and children. God often uses them to bring things to my attention. Listen to those who are the closest to you. They can help you keep your "blind spots" covered.

I ask myself, is it sugar levels, lack of sleep or medication? Or is it just me wanting to get my way? The Lord will show us, (especially through others, if we will listen) when it is a temper tantrum or when it is something off balance. So many things affect our moods, but ultimately we still have a choice whether to correct it or tolerate it.

Offense or unforgiveness is another door that we need to keep closed at all cost. We need to keep our hearts free of any offense. Right now, it may be easy for you to get offended. Eventually, through habitual practice, it should become difficult to offend you. Whether the offense is intentional or unintentional, it is vitally important that you keep your heart free of any bitterness or resentment. Forgive quickly and forgive often. Offense will open the door for so much mental instability and aguish. It is not worth holding a grudge or holding unforgiveness. Christ has forgiven us, we should freely and quickly forgive others as He has. The thought of the Father not forgiving us because we do not forgive others saddens me, because it separates me from Him, by choice. I need God's forgiveness every day and seek His mercy.

Keep your heart full of love. Seek peace with all men. Strive to enter into God's rest and, most of all, close those doors. Keep them closed so that you may stay free and bring others to freedom.

Prayer: It is for freedom that You set me free, Lord. Show me any places that I have given opportunity to the devil. Thank You for setting me free from guilt, anger, bitterness, resentment and unforgiveness. I forgive all who have offended me and thank You for forgiving me.

———◆———

Affirmation
I am free to set others free. I will not be entangled in bondage again. I resist the devil and he will run.

———◆———

Additional scriptures:

"So humble yourselves before God. Resist the devil and he will flee from you" (Jas 4.7).

Put on all of God's armor that you will be able to stand firm against all strategies of the devil. For we are not fighting against flesh and blood enemies, but against evil rulers and authorities of the unseen world, against mighty powers in this dark world and against evil spirits in the heavenly places. (Eph. 6.11, 12)

Dear friends, never take revenge. Leave that to the righteous anger of God. For the Scriptures say, "I will take revenge, I will pay them back," says the Lord. Instead, if your enemies are hungry, feed them. If they are thirsty, give them something to drink.... Don't let evil conquer you, but conquer evil by doing good. (Rom. 12.19-21)

But when you are praying, first forgive anyone you are holding a grudge against, so that your Father in heaven will forgive your sins, too." (Mark 11.26)

"So Christ has truly set us free. Now make sure that you stay free, and don't get tied up again in slavery to the law. (Gal. 5.1)

You Are Going to Make It!

Now all glory to God, who is able to keep you from falling away and
will bring you with great joy into his glorious presence without a
single fault. All glory to him alone who is God, our Savior through
Jesus Christ our Lord. All glory, majesty, power, and authority are his
before all time, and in the present, and beyond all time!

~JUDE 24, 25

YOU ARE GOING to make it!

Whatever you are going through, if it is depression, a manic episode, a psychotic episode: whatever. You are going to make it through by the grace of God.

You may be thinking, "How?" By living one day at a time and by trusting God each hour and each day. It may not be easy, but God is with you and He has every resource in Heaven and Earth available to you.

You may be in the hospital now or you may be alone in your home. Wherever you may be, God has given you a promise that He will present you faultless before His presence with exceeding joy. Remember that He is not distraught about where you are right now. He is completely aware and wanting to love you right where you are.

You have hope and hope will not let you down (Rom. 5.3-5). Hang on to your hope and don't let it go. It is an anchor to your soul. Do not be weary, your change is going to come (Job 14.14). The hardest part is expectantly waiting on God. Find out what you need to do while you are waiting.

Your warfare is to eat right, get plenty of rest, exercise and stay connected to a good church. It may be difficult for you to read huge amounts of your Bible, but read small verses of scripture. Always keep your prayers simple. Know that God hears them. Know that He cares about you. Pray your way through the day. Sing your way through the day. If you are at work, then do it quietly. Even if you are at home, you can sing and pray as you clean.

Right now I am in a season in my life where I have to fight boredom and idleness. I have to fight off isolation as well. Isolation and boredom will soon wear on me and begin to bring me down. So I reach out to others and try to keep my mind occupied and busy. You may have lost interest in things you used to do, some hobbies or outlet for you. Try to re-engage those hobbies or interests. Try to find a new past time that will give you an outlet for stress and stimulation. Try to get involved with an activity in your church for socialization and support. For me, it is being in our choir at church.

Remind yourself that God is with you always and that He will never leave you. He will never forsake you. One day you will look back and see all the many treasures that God has deposited in you. Not just for you, but for others. Everything that you experience will be a testimony of God's grace and love for you. Don't waste anything. God won't. Through every trial buy gold tried in the fire from Him (Rev. 3.18). Know that you will come through richer than when you went in.

Here is one final word of encouragement,

...Do not be afraid, for I have ransomed you. I have called you by name, you are mine. When you go through deep waters, I will be with you, when you go through rivers of difficulty, you will not drown. When you walk through the fire of oppression, you will not be burned up, the flames will not consume you. (Is. 43.1, 2)

Be encouraged today. You will make it through.

Prayer: Lord, thank You for being with me. Thank You for keeping me from stumbling. You will present me faultless before Your presence in glory. Thank You for Your grace. In Jesus' name, Amen.

———•———

Affirmation
I will make it through the fire and the flood.
I am more than a conqueror.

———•———

Scriptures to meditate on:

"I, the Lord, have called you to demonstrate my righteousness. I will take you by the hand and guard you…" (Isa. 42.6)

"Do not be afraid or discouraged. For the Lord will personally go ahead of you. He will be with you, he will neither fail you nor abandon you." (Deut. 31.8)

"No, despite all these things, overwhelming victory is ours through Christ, who loved us." (Rom. 8.37)

So God has given both his promise and his oath. These two things are unchangeable because it is impossible for God to lie. Therefore, we who have fled to him for refuge can have great confidence as we hold to the hope that lies before us. This hope is a strong and trustworthy anchor for our souls. It leads us through the curtain into God's inner sanctuary. (Heb. 6.18, 19)

It is Done!

"...despite all of these things, overwhelming victory is ours through Christ, who loved us."

~*ROMANS 8.37*

IT ALL BEGINS at Calvary where Jesus died for our sins, because of God's love.

"*For God loved the world so much that he gave his one and only Son, so that everyone who believes in him will not perish but have eternal life.*" (John 3.16)

The struggle is real but God has given us His power to overcome every lie of the devil. Through every wrestling match we have in our minds, Jesus gives us overwhelming victory because of His love.

Our victory began when Jesus shouted, "It is finished!" on the cross. He had fought and won the victory over death, hell and the grave with that victory shout. We can give that shout too when we are in the midst of a battle over our minds and when we are tearing down strongholds and mindsets in our thinking.

When our minds are filled with thoughts of fear, doubt and hopelessness, we have to believe that Jesus Christ has saved us and that we are safe in His love. It is easy to begin to think that we no longer belong to God because of feelings. We feel lost, without hope and unloveable. Because of the anger that was in my home growing up, my first thought is that God is angry with me. But recently God gave me a picture of this scripture. It was of me being in His embrace and, although the enemy was trying to separate me or pull me from His embrace, Jesus was holding me tightly.

"I cling to you. Your strong right hand holds me securely." (Ps. 68.8)

When I am in the midst of a psychotic break, my feelings are all over the place. The anxiety is high and I feel like I'm in a battle that I can never win, but the truth of the matter is that I have already won through Christ's sacrifice. I have to embrace the cross as He embraces me. The best thing I can do is to just be still and allow God to fight for me. It seems simple, but it is the hardest thing to do and I fail at it often. We can thank God that He has given us the victory through His resurrection power.

This resurrection life you received from God is not a timid, grave-tending life. It's adventurously expectant, greeting God with a childlike "What's next, Papa?" God's Spirit touches our spirits and confirms who we really are. We know who he is, and we know who we are: Father and children. And we know we are going to get what's coming to us—an unbelievable inheritance! We go through exactly what Christ goes through. If we go through the hard times with him, then we're certainly going to go through the good times with him! (Rom. 8. 15-17, MSG)

This passage makes me happy because it reminds me to whom I belong and that I'm God's child. When we suffer mental anguish, we are suffering as Christ did and will be partakers of His glory. To me, the best part of our suffering is the fellowship in the midst of it.

"I want to know Christ and experience the mighty power that raised him from the dead. I want to suffer with him, sharing in his death." (Phil. 3.10)

All the singing and praying we do in the midst of the storm is just to remind us that we are His and that He is right here with us, through it all.

My journey began at the crucifixion and resurrection of Jesus Christ, and because of Him I see the purpose of much of my suffering. He promises to work everything out for my good because of my love for Him and because I am called for a purpose.

We were given this hope when we were saved. (If we already have something, we don't need to hope for it. But if we look forward to something we don't yet have, we must wait patiently and confidently.) (Rom. 8.24, 25)

Hope is our mainstay. We have it when we believe in Jesus Christ for our salvation. Without Him there is no hope. With Him everything is ours~ hope, peace, joy and righteousness. It all begins and ends with Him. He is the Alpha and Omega. He is good and merciful and full of grace and love. He still disciplines us, but He is always kind and loving.

If you haven't begun your walk with Jesus Christ yet, begin with Him today. He will change all your tomorrows and deliver you from all the mistakes of your past. When you come to Him, He forgives all of our sins and forgets them forever.

If you are suffering from depression, PTSD, anxiety disorder or anything that causes mental anguish, Jesus is the One for you. He is for everyone but I think He has a special, deep love for those of us who suffer mentally.

So begin with Jesus Christ and you will begin with victory, regardless of feelings of fear, anxiety, helplessness or hopelessness. We can know the truth and be free from death through His incomprehensible love for us.

If you would like to begin your journey with Him, you can pray this prayer to begin all prayers:

Prayer: Lord Jesus, I believe You came to save me and that You love me with an everlasting love. I thank You for paying the price for my salvation and eternal life. I receive your free gift of grace as I ask You to be Lord of my life. I thank You for the victory and for my relationship with You and the Father. Thank You for making me Yours and I have made You mine. May I walk and serve You all the days of my life. Thank You for Your promise to stay with me through thick and thin. In Jesus Name, Amen.

———◆———

Affirmation
I am victorious because of God's love for me
and nothing can separate me from it.

———◆———

Scriptures to meditate on:

"The Lord will work out his plans for my life—for your faithful love, O Lord, endures forever. Don't abandon me, for you made me." (Ps. 138.8)

"For since our friendship with God was restored by the death of his Son while we were still his enemies, we will certainly be saved through the life of his Son.

So now we can rejoice in our wonderful new relationship with God because our Lord Jesus Christ has made us friends of God" (Rom. 5.10, 11).

Coping Skills

BELOW I HAVE a few coping skills that have helped through the years and continue to help as my capacity continues to grow. Here's the thing about coping skills. You have to practice them before or when you don't need them so that they become second nature to you when you are under stress, having an anxiety or panic attack, or a flashback of some sort. Stress is always the main component of anxiety or even relapses in drug additions.

I work in a very stressful job where I have to make good decisions when I am dealing with someone who is in a mental health crisis, having suicidal thoughts or anxiety. I also live in the Rockies where the air is thin so I need more oxygen to my brain whenever I feel I am making decisions based on emotions rather than logic. So what I have found is that breathing works well for me when I am stressed.

Rather than breathe in my nose, then out through the mouth, I find that breathing a deep belly breath where my belly grows or really deeply, then hold it for three seconds, then out through my nose.

Science has proven that it only takes 30 seconds to relieve stress so I have learned to stop, take a breath, and think about what is stressing me out. For instance, trying to find my keys on the way out the door when I'm running late really stresses me to the point where I get frustrated, then panicked, then acting on that emotion. First of all, I have gotten to the point where I can recognize my physical response to the stress that is causing the anxiety. Then, I can go to what has become second nature to me which is taking a breath. This also works when I feel rushed at work and need to think on my feet. I don't necessarily have to close my eyes but sometimes I do.

I also have a journal at work (I don't really care who reads it) that I will actually pull out and start jotting down prayers and requests from the Lord or that I will take with me on my break to help me process a my thoughts after a difficult or emotional client.

When you believe in God, prayer is the only way you can stay connected to the actual source and that is why it is probably the best coping skill to use because the Holy Spirit can give us wisdom when we ask to include taking a break to eat, taking a nap to rest or drinking water. He just shows us how to live skillfully.

Here is a brief list of others I use for anxiety or depression:

Prayer

We sometimes use prayer as a Christmas list where we ask for whatever we want and God is OK with that. He wants us to come to Him about everything. But, as our desire to know Him grows we get to the point where we want to be like Him and ask Him to help us to be like Him. So, I begin my prayer time with a simple request:

"Search me, O God, and know my heart; test me and know my anxious thoughts. Point out anything in me that offends you, and lead me along the path of everlasting life" (Ps. 139. 23, 24).

Prayer is our lifeline. It is how we communicate with God and Him alone. I am careful not to refer to God in generalities, yet, His name and the descriptions of Him is more than we can number. The true and living God sent his Son as Emanuel, God with us, who left glory and born in the flesh to make a way for us to have a relationship with Him.

"Don't fret or worry. Instead of worrying, pray. Let petitions and praises shape your worries into prayers, letting God know your concerns. Before you know it, a sense of God's wholeness, everything coming together for good, will come and

settle you down. It's wonderful what happens when Christ displaces worry at the center of your life" Phil. 4.6,7 (MSG)

Our relationship with God is what brings peace and wholeness in our lives, spiritually, emotionally, mentally and physically.

People all over the world pray to different people or things and for different reasons. One thing that separates Christianity from all is Jesus Christ was born man and Creator from the beginning.

"In the beginning the Word already existed.
    The Word was with God,
    and the Word was God.
He existed in the beginning with God.
God created everything through him,
    and nothing was created except through him.
The Word gave life to everything that was created,[a]
    and his life brought light to everyone.
The light shines in the darkness,
    and the darkness can never extinguish it" John 1.1-4

He is all God and all man. He's the One who knows how to pray for us because He walked on the earth as one of us, yet without a sinful nature.

So the Word became human and made his home among us. He was full of unfailing love and faithfulness John 1.14.

How powerful is that?! How wonderful! I can walk with Jesus as my God, Creator and Friend. Prayers of all kinds becomes the language of our lives. His Word is near us as He speaks to us through His Spirit and listens. Through the Cross, He is near us and far, far away. He's as near as the breath we breathe.

I have a prayer journal everywhere I go because I like to write them throughout the day and it stays between me and Jesus. I know that He hears me where no one else can go. Deep in my heart.

Forgiveness
Forgive quickly and forgive often.

*"If you forgive those who sin against you, your heavenly Father will forgive you.
15 But if you refuse to forgive others, your Father will not forgive your sins (Matt.
6.14).*

Love...
Doesn't keep score of the sins of others,
Trust steadily in God,
hope unswervingly,
love extravagantly.
And the best of the three is love. 1 Cor. 13.7, 13 (MSG).

"The first to apologize is the bravest
The first to forgive is the strongest"
~ Pastor Boyd Brady, New Life Church, Colorado Springs, CO

Sometimes, it's helpful to just write a letter to the person who hurt you. You can decide whether to give it to them or not.

Exercise
You only need a little just to be consistent. Just a 20 minute walk everyday helps. I had to go easy on this. I had been taking a medication that was causing a lot of weight gain so I thought I would go and hire a personal trainer. I think the trainer was focused on losing weight fast by first building muscle that would burn more calories and I was on a low fat, high protein diet. I would pay $30 a session and go three days a week. What I didn't realize and my husband did was that it triggered a Manic episode. It's true. When we build muscle it increases our metabolism. At the time I went from slow to being very high all of a sudden. It was too much of a push. The result was a Manic episode because by body started metabolizing my medications, so I

probably needed to increase the dosage to keep up with how fast it was burning up my medication.

We only need to exercise a little every day. Our society is so focused on body image. It's an obsession that drives us to do unhealthy things. Be happy. I would rather be chunky, happy and not depressed than skinny, mean, depressed or manic because of an imbalance in my medications and brain function. Be ok being healthy and whole body conscious more than weight conscious.

Organization

Taking time to think about where to put things that you use regularly helps reduce stress. It's like getting everything out that you need to cook a meal before you start so you aren't hunting for a cup of sugar.

Lists help me and having the right containers, office supplies (yep, labels) and organization furniture helps, too. I try to organize the night before, but it's difficult for me to incorporated into my night time ritual so I might only be able to make a list for the morning and that's if I'm having a morning where I can get up early enough to do everything on the list.

Lists also help to organize our time. I have to put appointments into one calendar that I can have with me, in written form or electronically. I still have to take time to write To Do Lists make them in 30 minute intervals. Example:

8:00am – brush teeth
8:15am – Coffee & Devotional (it would be great if I ate too)
8:45am – Iron clothes (might do it the night before or beginning of the week
9:15am – Shower/dress (Sometimes part of my sleep ritual)
9:30am – Clean kitchen
10:00am – Get dressed
10:30am – Leave for work
✓ Lunch/snack
✓ Cell Phone

✓ Purse
✓ Sweater
✓ Keys
7:00p – Take medication
9:00 – House down. No electronics/TVs on and everyone is in their rooms
10:00 – Get ready for bed
✓ Get into PJs
✓ Watch "Golden Girls"/"Fraser"/"Bernie Mac" (2 ep.)
✓ 11:00p – Meds should kick in and it's "Nighty-Night"

"Sweet and Sour Game"

I picked up this game from my girls. When they were little and bored they would go outside and wave at the cars passing by. If they waved back, they were "Sweet". If not, then they were "Sour". Sometimes, they would come in and report to me how many they had of each.

I struggle with social anxiety off and on and for the most part do my best to avoid crowded social functions or any kind of store that is crowded. I could care less about sales events because of the crowds. During Christmas, I shop at stores that are open 24 hours and go shopping at 10pm or even midnight so no crowds. But every so often it is unavoidable.

It was during my devotional time that I felt God reminding me to smile. That was my job. But, then the Social Scientist in me decided to do an experiment. The thesis was, Will I feel better if I smiled?

The game is simple. I smile at someone and if they smile back then they are "Sweet" and I think maybe I made their day. If they're "Sour" I am thankful that my day wasn't as bad as theirs and maybe their situation was worse than mine. Of course, this is not appropriate for every public place so your church might be a good place to practice this skill. I play this game to get my mind off myself and being self-conscious.

Random Acts of Kindness

When I am having stressful day I might go to the drive through for coffee and pay the order for the person behind me. I only budget a few dollars on payday. It's $20. It gets my mind off myself and, hopefully, makes that person's day. It doesn't have to involve money. I always keep a pack of cards for all occasions around and if I think of someone at work or in my sphere of influence I might write a card anonymously with words of encouragement.

> *"Jesus said, "'Love the Lord your God with all your passion and prayer and intelligence.' This is the most important, the first on any list. But there is a second to set alongside it: 'Love others as well as you love yourself.' These two commands are pegs; everything in God's Law and the Prophets hangs from them" Matt. 22. 37-40.*

My conclusion was that it's really not about me. The whole world does not revolve around us. It's easy to become so self-absorbed that we become lost in our own little world. When we do things sacrificially and out of love for God and others, it transforms us into brave people instead of fearful ones.

Celebrate everything!

You're worth it! Try to find a way to reward yourself when you are able to function or accomplish a small goal. You might want to do it at the end of the day after time to reflect. You can celebrate small accomplishments and feel empowered to pray and plan the next day, surrendering both to God's sovereignty. Thanking Him in everything.

> *"Celebrate God all day, every day. I mean, revel in him! Make it as clear as you can to all you meet that you're on their side, working with them and not against them. Help them see that the Master is about to arrive. He could show up any minute!" Phil. 4.4,5. (MSG)*

Journal intentionally

Many people think that journaling means documenting all the things that are going wrong in their life or just a record of what happened throughout the day. I use David and some of his psalms as a good example of journaling. It is often conversational as prayers directed towards God and start as a complaint or request, then he later turns his focus towards God through thanksgiving and praise for who He is and all he has done.

There are three ways I journal. I have a prayer journal, a "Yay Me" journal and a gratitude journal. I might not have three separate journals but I choose one of these ways to journal when I do. I also have a journal of inspirational quotes, promises in scripture and words of encourage the Lord may speak to me, even notes from a sermon that I could apply to what was going on in my life at the time. I sometimes fold the pages of my favorites so I can refer back to them as reminders. Then, when I am struggling with symptoms I can look back and actually gain something from them and they always seem to be exactly what I needed to hear. I also like those spiral bound journals that have scripture verses on the bottom of the page and I fold the pages of promises I need to remember and meditate on.

I think journaling is kind of like the ant who works all summer to save up for the winter. When winter comes he has something to feed on. Likewise, when I am in a normal mood I try to journal more than usual because when winter comes and I am in a depressive mood and not feel like journaling, I can look back and still be encouraged and have something to feed my faith and hope. It sustains me through those winter or depressive seasons. They remind of times when I wasn't feeling depressed and gives me hope that I can be there again. It's all temporary and will pass.

Keep it Movin'

It's like the law of Physics. What goes into motion, stays in motion. It's just a matter of starting. Then, you can gain some momentum that will take you through your storm.

Find at least one activity you can do daily, then weekly. Baby steps. For me, I needed to go to the library to get out of the house once a week. This is helpful when that Agoraphobia (fear of leaving the house) creep up on me or I'm isolating myself. I have a habit of making my bed when I get out of it or before I leave for work or go get my coffee in the morning. It's a little harder for me to get back into bed and go to sleep after I've brushed my teeth and for a few months I wasn't able to leave my room so I would lay across my bed and either read or even go to sleep but I would be OK with not getting back into bed. Once I made my bed I felt like I could resist the temptation and move on to brushing my teeth, then getting dressed, then leaving my room. Coffee is a good motivator to get out of my room.

Mindfulness/ Meditation
"May the words of my mouth and the **meditation** *of my heart be pleasing to you, O Lord, my rock and my redeemer" Ps. 19.14.*

Mindfulness and meditation terms used within the mental health community when it comes to spirituality. I have a problem with the concept of emptying your mind and focusing on energy, breathing, the universe and nature unless it is to focus on God's glory as Creator of everything.

Our focus has to be on God what Jesus says to us in His word and staying in the present when we are dreading the future. When we are in the present we can look at those things that are worrying us or overwhelming us.

This is the purpose of the scriptures in this book. I have had times where it was difficult to focus on anything, but sometimes there's a promise that God wants to remind us of that helps us put our trust and hope in Him and acknowledge that He's in control.

The other issue with mindfulness without Jesus Christ at the center is that we are susceptible to being drawn to and worshipping other things. Turning to our "inner self" only leads to deception, emptiness and darkness. Only the Holy Spirit through scripture can cleanse and bring light to our hearts and minds.

"The human heart is the most deceitful of all things, and desperately wicked. Who really knows how bad it is?"

(Jer. 17.9).

"For the word of God is alive and powerful. It is sharper than the sharpest two-edged sword, cutting between soul and spirit, between joint and marrow. It exposes our innermost thoughts and desires" (Heb 4.12).

Because of our sinful nature, we automatically have a tendency to remember the bad things in our past. We have to ask the Holy Spirit what we should focus on in the moment so He can work in us and transform us when He speaks to us through the Word of God.

The beautiful thing about focusing on God is that, even when He is correcting us about something in our life, it confirms that we belong to Him and that He loves us enough to deal with those things that will hurt us. Being mindful and quiet before God also means allowing Him to search our hearts and to change our way of thinking when His Spirit corrects a certain way of thinking or sinful practices. It can be a painful process when God searches our hearts and directs us to areas we need to work on.

"So don't feel sorry for yourselves. Or have you forgotten how good parents treat children, and that God regards you as his children?

My dear child, don't shrug off God's discipline,
but don't be crushed by it either.
It's the child he loves that he disciplines;
the child he embraces, he also corrects.

God is educating you; that's why you must never drop out. He's treating you as dear children. This trouble you're in isn't punishment; it's training, the normal experience of children. Only irresponsible parents leave children to fend for themselves. Would you prefer an irresponsible God?

....But God is doing what is best for us, training us to live God's holy best. At the time, discipline isn't much fun. It always feels like it's going against the grain. Later, of course, it pays off handsomely, for it's the well-trained who find themselves mature in their relationship with God"
Heb 12:4-11 (MSG)

Our relationship with God should be the center of our meditations and mindfulness practices. Our goal should be to be strengthened in our inner man through the Holy Spirit, know the love of Christ that is beyond our comprehension and that He would make His home in our hearts. Paul prayed:

"I pray that from his glorious, unlimited resources he will empower you with inner strength through his Spirit. Then Christ will make his home in your hearts as you trust in him. Your roots will grow down into God's love and keep you strong. And may you have the power to understand, as all God's people should, how wide, how long, how high, and how deep his love is. May you experience the love of Christ, though it is too great to understand fully. Then you will be made complete with all the fullness of life and power that comes from God (Eph. 3.16-19).

We live in a world full of distractions and it takes practice to pull aside and focus. There are some coping skills that suggest distraction as a way to cope with depression. Usually, people use TV as a way to distract or video games. But these tend to help numb us and repress emotional wounds that we'd rather not deal with. After hours on our couch, we look back and realize that we have wasted the day. And, of course, at least for me, those emotions, hurts or memories return as soon as the TV goes off and it's quiet. So it ends up being only temporary relief and delays the inevitable. Not to mention, it is addictive. To be honest, the quiet used to frighten me because it often forced me to surrender to something the Holy Spirit wants to deal with me about. I would think I was in trouble or God was going to ask me to become a Missionary to Africa. Nothing could be further from the truth. If possible, I try to abstain from TV every Monday.

I tend to think that rather than adding another distract from the what might be the root of my emotional pain, we should displace those negative thoughts with what is true about ourselves, God and those around us so we are more encouraging than critical.

"Summing it all up, friends, I'd say you'll do best by filling your minds and meditating on things true, noble, reputable, authentic, compelling, gracious— the best, not the worst; the beautiful, not the ugly; things to praise, not things to curse. Put into practice what you learned from me, what you heard and saw and realized. Do that, and God, who makes everything work together, will work you into his most excellent harmonies" (Phil. 4.7, 8).

When I did get quiet I realized that I began to expect to hear God speak to my heart or put a scripture on my mind. Sometimes, I would think of one word, like joy, then go to my Concordance in my Bible and look up all the scriptures on joy. Now, I would look forward to my quiet time and would wait expectantly for a word or a song that touched my heart or just acknowledge the fact that God was right there with me whether I "felt" Him or not.

"Rest in the LORD, and wait patiently for Him" (Ps. 37:7).

After learning how to be quiet, I started waiting expectantly for God to show me more and more about who is was and His great love for me. But, now I realize that it was my time to recharge my battery when I felt depleted. I found that my time with the Lord could be just listening to music, daydreaming, reflection, writing a card to a friend, calling a friend who is sick, or even planning out my day with Him in mind. I usually feel renewed, refreshed and ready for the day.

> *Have you never heard?*
> *Have you never understood?*
> *The LORD is the everlasting God,*
> *the Creator of all the earth.*

He never grows weak or weary.
   No one can measure the depths of his understanding
He gives power to the weak
   and strength to the powerless…
But those who trust in the Lord will find new strength.
   They will soar high on wings like eagles.
They will run and not grow weary.
   They will walk and not faint " (Is. 40:28, 29, 31).

When I do watch TV, I am very selective. Part of my ritual after a stressful day was to eat a bowl of my favorite cereal and watch my favorite Sitcoms. Being very selective about what I watch is important and I am aware of how what I'm watching affects me.

One mindfulness exercise that helps me when I have racing thoughts or having trouble getting to sleep is the five senses exercise.

1. First, find five things you can *see* – you can name them out loud or in your head if you are in public or if it helps you to focus better and displace negative thoughts.
2. Find five things you can *hear* – you might want to keep your eyes closed to listen
3. Find five things you can *taste* – Sometimes you can taste your last meal. This really takes concentration. If you can't come up with five, then try using a piece of candy or ice and describe it in your head. For instance, a Jolly Rancher might be described as hard, sour, a little salty, wet and so one.
4. Find five things you can *smell* – You want to do your best to focus on what you smell at that very moment. I might be someone's cologne, the city, car. Try to narrow it down and wait for it. Outside is great. This might be where Aromatherapy might be helpful or lighting a scented candle. I usually have a lotion with me, Eucalyptus and Peppermint Stress Reliever lotion. I will take three deep breaths. Breathing is the most effective and convenient way to relieve stress and engage the

present. Smell is very powerful so finding something that reminds you of better times or happy memory might be uplifting. Doing some breathing in the shower with your favorite bath soap helps.

5. Find five things you can ***touch*** – I learned this years ago when I was having a very bad psychotic episode. I called my church and thankfully at that time there was a certified Therapist who could walk me through this.

She just asked me to find five things I could touch and tell her out loud. She told me it should be five things I could feel right then at that moment. I remember telling her I felt my legs touching the chair, my bottom on the chair, my hands on the arms of the chair and my feet in my shoes. Afterwards, I could finally listen to what she was saying and able to tell her what was going on and how I felt at the time.

After finding five things each sense, then try 4, then 3, 2, 1 thing. Don't worry if you can't. Sometimes I can only find five things I can see and stick to one thing of the other senses.

Listening to Music & Singing

Music is a global language that speaks to our hearts. It sets the mood for our thoughts and feelings. I think we often choose "Theme Songs" for the seasons of our lives. Songs that convey a message of healing, hope and restoration. I think God has a playlist of worship songs He loves to hear from us.

"He has given me a new song to sing, a hymn of praise to our God" (Ps. 40.3).

"I will sing a new song to you, O God!" (Ps. 144.9).

Music is very attached to our memories, good or bad. I have songs that I play over and over again.

Singing in a choir at church is so therapeutic and keeps us from depression, especially SAD. Singing in a Christmas or Easter program with a choir you get two-for-one at the same time. You can sing to lift your spirits and you can come together with a common goal and create songs that can uplift others.

When I was in a choir, the Praise and Worship leaders would give us CDs to listen to new songs for the week. One leader said when we play and hear a song seven times, it gets into our head, heart and mind. Furthermore, humming and singing actually causes vibrations throughout our jaw, brain and skull and effects our mood, emotions and memory. I think that's why kids can learn almost anything when it's set to music. Find songs that set your life to music in the direction you want it to go. If your marriage is being challenged, stay away from the sad love songs and focus on the timeless love songs of devotion and sincere adoration. I want my worship music to revolve around what I want to express personally.

Music can also be used to help with auditory hallucinations. It should be music we know and that we can sing to. I used to think that if someone just listened to soothing, instrumental or classical music, it would help redirect our thinking and distract from the distressing thoughts or voices. The key is not that it's soothing, but that you have to engage your memory to think about the words that are familiar.

Personally, I can't listen to songs with words I don't know when I am having psychotic symptoms. I tend to hear the wrong lyrics and that the music is directed to me. What helps me is to have a playlist that I can sing with and another that I can listen to without words and lyrics to confuse me.

Corporate worship is imperative. Being able to sit in the midst of others who share the same faith and lift up our voices corporately is powerful when we don't have the words to say or know the songs to sing.

Playing "happy tunes" don't necessarily do the trick either, because sometimes it just grates on our nerves. Trying to use music to help us to just "snap out of it" sort of defeats the purpose of music as a form of expression of deep emotion. Be honest.

"Singing cheerful songs to a person with a heavy heart is like taking someone's coat in cold weather or pouring vinegar in a wound" (Prov 25.20).

We can't use music to get us happy as if our Father only accepts us a certain way. I think we avoid songs full of emotion and confession because they might make us feel uncomfortable and we feel guilty when we aren't jumping up and down at church, but just want to sit and enjoy being with God and His people.

Fellowship, Communion & Friendship

Some people who struggle with Depression stop going to church altogether because of shame and the feeling that it's our job to make sure others feel comfortable around us. When they don't, then we might get some comments or simply be ignored because some people might ask how you're doing and not really stop to listen. Then, some do and feel awkward because they don't know what to say.

This may be the case with you, but I've learned that Church was the safest place for me to be. I know we now have internet, but as the Day of Jesus' return approaches, I find that there is safety when I allow myself to be vulnerable. There are some things that happen when we are as one Body of Christ and His Bride that we can't get when we are worshipping alone.

"Confess your sins to each other and pray for each other so that you may be healed. The earnest prayer of a righteous person has great power and produces wonderful results" (Jms. 5.16).

There's healing when we participate in corporate prayer and worship. When we pray for one another and are vulnerable enough to disclose our struggles.

The 1st Century Church went from house to house breaking bread together and sharing meals and testimonies of faith with one another. Coming to the Lord's table as God's people in remembrance of our Savior's sacrifice and of a time when we will all be part of the marriage supper of the Lamb is so powerful.

I am currently attending a church where we take Communion almost every Sunday. Growing up it was only done on the 1st Sunday of the month. But our Pastor believes that we should constantly be brought to the table and reminded of the fact that we can only put our trust in the Lamb of God who gave His life for us. I never want to forget and taking Communion motivates me even if I barely make it through the door.

I would like to stress this just a little more. We should attend a church that has sound doctrine when it comes to our faith in Jesus Christ. When looking for a church, their mission should line up with a clear profession of faith in Jesus Christ. Nowadays, sermons can be seen on a screen outside in a café or living room time area outside the Sanctuary if you are uncomfortable with crowds.

Sometimes, going to church every week just can't happen, but you can meet with other families or couples for frozen yogurt, coffee or dinner.

The main point is that God never designed us to walk this life utterly alone. He said He won't leave us or abandon us and one way that He shows He's with us is through the love of His people.

Diet/Sleep

Drink water! Drink water! Drink water!

I can't stress that enough. Water is connected to Electrolytes in our body and helps everything else function well.

When I was younger, one of the things that caused the imbalance was my fasting from food and not drinking water. I would go on 40 day fasts from food and not realized that it was crucial to drink water. I also didn't recognize that I had actually stopped wanting to live and that my not eating might have been my way of slowly starving myself to death. Suicidal thoughts can be wrapped in many different things.

I don't fast from food anymore. I normally fast from TV or electronics, but I have to drink at least 64 to 94 glasses of water a day. It helps every organ in my body.

Water helps keep the toxins out of your body. My husband will ask me every once-in –a-while if I had been drinking water because he could smell the toxins in my breath and in the odor of toxins that coming out of my pores.

Water also helps lessen some of the damage that some medications have on our organs. In my job, water and oxygen are crucial when it comes to making good decisions in a stressful situation. Here are some other things you can incorporate into your diet:

- Stay away from low-carb diets. Lack of carbohydrates affect our moods and energy. Nuts, beans and grains work really well for both blood sugar levels and fiber.
- For sleep, you can take Calcium/Magnesium. You need both because the Magnesium helps your body absorb the calcium. A glass of milk will help
- A half of a chicken/sandwich before bed to help with sugar levels through the night or to provide a natural sleep aid
- Melatonin helps with sleep

Me Time

Time for ourselves when raising three little girls under the age of five and then starting all over again with two more boys is next to impossible, but self-care is crucial.

First, I had to find out what that looked like because I had forgotten things liked to do for relaxation and recreation. I would crave huge amounts of time off that I could never realistically pull off and became frustrated with what I could pull off. So here are some of my little moments that I steal throughout the day that sort of add up to a few hours sometimes by the end of the week:

- Take a shower with your favorite body wash, in the dark with a candle lit.
- Sing in the shower
- Sit in a chair on a porch or in the drive way and watch the sunset
- Have a cup of tea with your favorite tea cups and saucers
- Bring someone coffee-in-bed. I used to do for my kids on occasion
- Have dessert each night
- Make a candle light dinner with soup and crackers
- Have an indoor/outdoor picnic with the kids for lunch. We did this when the boys were little and sit under a tree in our front yard
- Put your favorite lotion on hands and feet before bed each night

- Take a short walk. I took them several times a day but only about five houses down the street and back. It helped.
- Sit and read at the library

The idea is to find out what you really like spending time doing and do it. No matter how much or little you do, engage. It makes all the difference in the world.

Songs of Hope

Songs

Avant. "Sailing". *Sailing.* 2009. MP3

Bethel College Chapel Band. "Love Came Down." *Love Came Down.* n.d. CD.

Cook, Amanda. "You Make Me Brave (Live)." *You Make Me Brave.* Bethel Music. n.d. MP3.

Desperation Band. "Amazed." *Songs 4 Worship 50.* Various Artists. 2009. CD.

Dimarco, Kristen. "It is well (Live)." *You Make Me Brave.* Bethel Music, n.d. MP3.

Fortune, James. "Holy is Our God." *James Fortune and Fiya,* n.d. MP3.

Jobe, Kari. "Here." *Where I find you: Christmas Edition.* n.d., MP3

Franklin, Kirk. "Better." *Hero.* 2005. MP3

Franklin, Kirk. "Declaration. (This is it)." *The Fight of My Life.* 2007. MP3

Franklin, Kirk. "Hide Me." *The* Essential *Kirk Franklin.* 2011. MP3

Franklin, Kirk. "I Smile." *Hello Fear.* 2009. MP3

Frizzel Gretzinger, Steffany. "You Know Me". Bethel Music: The Loft Sessions, 2012, MP3

Johnson, Brian and Jenn. "A Little Longer." Bethel Music, 2012. MP3

Johnson, Jenn. "Come to Me." The Loft Sessions. Bethel Music, 2012. MP3.

King Cole, Nate. "Smile." The Nate King Cole Story. Capitol Records, n.d. MP3. CD

MercyMe. "Word of God Speak." Cry Out to Jesus. Gilead Baptist Church. 2006. MP3.

McClurkin, Donnie. "We Fall Down." Live in London and More.., 2000. MP3.

McClurkin, Donnie. "Psalm 27." Live in London and More.., 2000. MP3.

Mullen, Teresa. "Draw Me in Your Presence - Instrumental." Jesus, Draw Me Close. Maranatha! Instrumental. 1998. MP3.

Reagan, Will. "Running in Circles." United Pursuit. Will Reagan, n.d. MP3.

Rodriguez, Freddy. "Wrap Me in Your Arms." Light in the Darkness, 2009. MP3.

Sinton, Matt. Bethel Music. "Give Me Jesus." Tides Live, 2014. MP3.

Walls Group. "Perfect People." Fast Forward, 2015. MP3.

Williams, Pharrell. "Happy." Despicable Me 2. (Original Motions Picture Soundtrack). Various Artists. 2013. CD.

Withers, Bill. "Lovely Day." Discover Bill Withers. 2007. CD.

Albums

Bethel Music. *You Make Me Brave. Bethel Music.* 2014, CD.

Bethel Music. *The Loft Sessions.* Bethel Music. 2012. CD.

Unite, Hillsong. *Empires.* Hillsong. 2015. CD.

Winans, CeCe. *Throne Room, n.d.* CD.

Maranatha! Instrumental. *Jesus Draw Me Close.* 1998. CD.

Videos – Youtube

Bethel Music. https://www.youtube.com/watch?v=vGnpWo9SLuk&list=PLWgoyvQZz Uzjo158I0rVCD7teb7WCzZ2u. *The Loft Sessions.* Bethel Music, 2012.YouTube.

Dncn4myjesus. https://www.youtube.com/watch?v=pyLJlkYv8hw *"A Little Longer"* with the *"Passion of the Christ".* YouTube.

Ann3Nas. https://www.youtube.com/watch?v=jLS8fxHNpOQ *Through the Many Winters – Michael McDonald.* , 2012. Youtube.

Instrumentals

Botti, Chris, Ma, Yo-Yo. "Cinema Paradiso." *Chris Botti in Boston,* 2009. MP3.

Lorber, Jeff. "Requiem For Gandalf." *He Had a Hat.* 2007. CD

Maranatha! Instrumental. *Jesus Draw Me Close*. 1998. CD

Tankard, Ben. "Morning Prayer." *Full Tank*. Ben Tankard. 2012. CD.

———

Book List

Hager, Linda Carruth and W. David M.D. "Stress and the Woman's Body". 1998. Paperback.

Hart, Archibald, Dr. D. "Adrenaline and Stress: The Exciting New Breakthrough That Helps You Overcome Stress Damage. Word Publishing. 1995. Paperback.

McGee, Robert. "The Search for Significance: Seeing Your True Worth Through God's Eyes. Thomas Nelson. 1998. Paperback.

McGee, Robert. "The Search for Significance Workbook: Building Your Self-Worth Through God's Truth. Thomas Nelson. 1998, 2003.

McVey, Steve. "Grace Walk: What You've Always Wanted in the Christian Life. Harvest House Publishers. 1995. Paperback.